T0032559

HOW TO FOCUS

ANCIENT WISDOM FOR MODERN READERS

■ ■ ■ ■

HOW TO FOCUS

■ ■ ■ ■ ■

A Monastic Guide for an Age of Distraction

John Cassian

*Selected, translated,
and introduced by Jamie Kreiner*

PRINCETON UNIVERSITY PRESS

PRINCETON AND OXFORD

Published by Princeton University Press
41 William Street, Princeton, New Jersey 08540
99 Banbury Road, Oxford OX2 6JX

press.princeton.edu

Library of Congress Cataloging-in-Publication Data

Names: Cassian, John, author. | Kreiner, Jamie, translator.
Title: How to focus: a monastic guide for an age of distraction /
John Cassian; selected, translated, and introduced by Jamie Kreiner.
Description: Princeton: Princeton University Press, 2024. |
Series: Ancient wisdom for modern readers |
Includes bibliographical references.
Identifiers: LCCN 2023010545 (print) | LCCN 2023010546 (ebook) |
ISBN 9780691208084 (hardback) | ISBN 9780691250151 (ebook)
Subjects: LCSH: Attention—Early works to 1800. |
Distraction (Psychology)—Early works to 1800. |
Spiritual life—Early works to 1800.
Classification: LCC BR65.C32 E5 2024 (print) | LCC BR65.C32 (ebook) |
DDC 153.7/33—dc23/eng/20230703
LC record available at https://lccn.loc.gov/2023010545
LC ebook record available at https://lccn.loc.gov/2023010546

British Library Cataloging-in-Publication Data is available

Editorial: Rob Tempio and Chloe Coy
Production Editorial: Theresa Liu
Text Design: Pamela L. Schnitter
Jacket/Cover Design: Heather Hansen
Production: Erin Suydam
Publicity: Tyler Hubbert and Carmen Jimenez
Copyeditor: Kathleen Kageff

Jacket image: Upper Part of a Grave Stela with a
Deacon-Monk. © Dumbarton Oaks,
Byzantine Collection, Washington, DC.

This book has been composed in Stempel Garamond

Printed on acid-free paper. ∞

Printed in the United States of America

1 3 5 7 9 10 8 6 4 2

CONTENTS

INTRODUCTION

Distraction is not a new problem tied to our technology. It's something that people have struggled with for centuries, even at a time when books counted as newish devices and the main way to glance at the "clock" was to look outside at the sun. We're not the first to complain about how hard it is to concentrate, or even to moralize the issue. Christian monks in the late Roman Empire beat us to it. Their work required intense concentration, which made them all the more aware of how hard it was to master.[1]

Like many of their contemporaries, monks saw cognition as an activity that both expressed who they were and made them what they were.[2] Thinking about how to focus therefore amounted to thinking about how to live, as the person one wanted to be. And what

monks wanted, in late antiquity, was to dedicate their lives and attention to God and to their ethical obligations within a divinely ordered universe.

The problem was that the mind (like the self) is an inherently slippery thing. John Cassian, whose thoughts about thinking influenced centuries of monks, wrote in the 420s that the mind "gets pushed around by random distractions." It rifles through the past rather than staying fixed on the present. It thinks about dinner when it's supposed to be concentrating on a psalm. It careens haphazardly between stimuli. It falls asleep during the night prayers. It wonders what time it is when it's supposed to be buried in a book.

Many monks in Cassian's day blamed demons for their lapses.[3] These demons lurked all around them, shooting distracting thoughts at them that could cause serious harm if monks weren't quick to react. Cassian agreed that demons were part of the problem, but he was also sure that

distractedness was a human condition that could be mitigated by disciplining the mind, which involved examining and restructuring the conceptual, emotional, somatic, and social forces that were interlaced with monks' mental activities. A large portion of his *Collationes*—that is, *Consultations*, or *Conversations*, or (as it's usually translated) *The Conferences*—is dedicated to helping monks take up that training. As the historian and monk Columba Stewart has noted, "The question of focus is the single most important practical problem Cassian addresses in his monastic theology."[4] Although many elements of Cassian's late antique anthropology and cosmology are far from our own concepts of cognition, we share with him an interest in combatting distraction and focusing on the things that matter to us. And what Cassian can offer, as an expert who has both succeeded and failed to focus, is advice that is at once more sympathetic and more sophisticated than what we're used to.

CASSIAN AND HIS WORK

John Cassian was a monk who lived in the Roman Empire in the fourth and early fifth centuries CE.[5] These were still relatively early days in the history of Christian monasticism: Cassian was born in the 360s, as part of the generation that sought out the monastic pioneers in Egypt and the Levant who were old enough to be their parents and grandparents, to learn from them personally. The accounts that Cassian and others wrote about these encounters brought their role models international renown as the fathers and mothers of Christian monasticism. Cassian himself actually made it into that canon, too, alongside his personal heroes: he makes a cameo appearance in the immensely popular *Apophthegmata patrum* or *Sayings of the Desert Elders*, stories that circulated for centuries throughout Mesopotamia, the Mediterranean, and Europe.[6]

It's not certain where in the empire Cassian was born, but we do know that he joined his first

monastery in Bethlehem when he was in his twenties, with a close friend named Germanus. From there the two struck out to Scetis and other monastic communities in the Nile delta, where they spent around fifteen years interviewing and learning from monastic elders in the hopes of becoming better practitioners themselves. When Egyptian monasticism became roiled by debates about the teachings of Evagrius—a monk who deeply influenced Cassian's work, though Cassian never speaks of him directly—Cassian and Germanus fled to Constantinople and served in the ecclesiastical entourage of the imperial capital's archbishop, John Chrysostom. But Chrysostom was a divisive figure, too, and when he was deposed and exiled only a few years later, Cassian and Germanus traveled to Rome in an effort to defend him. Historians don't know what became of Germanus after that, but Cassian eventually moved to southern Gaul, by the 410s at the latest, when he would have been in his fifties. This was no

quiet provincial getaway. By the time Cassian arrived in Gaul, political authority at both the imperial and the local levels had been sharply contested in this region for a few decades. Cassian found that the Christians he met there, rich and influential Christians in particular, were hungry for stories of what he'd learned in Egypt, searching as they were for moral exemplars and authoritative models of leadership. So in the 420s he narrativized the most memorable conversations he'd had with Germanus and their Egyptian mentors and sculpted them into an argument for living ethically, day by day, while coming to terms with one's error-prone, ever-moving mind: this was the *Collationes*.

Given the sheer diversity of monastic models and forms of spiritual authority in late antiquity, it's all the more remarkable that the *Collationes*, together with Cassian's *De institutis coenobiorum* (*The Foundations of Monastic Communities*, better known as *The Institutes*), became such influential texts. One hagiographer tells us that Cassian's

writings inspired a young North African abbot named Fulgentius to set sail for Egypt in the later fifth century, to meet the holy monks whom he already saw as his "parents." But he never made it there, his hagiographer tells us: Fulgentius got so excited talking about Cassian's work at a dinner with the bishop of Syracuse that the bishop persuaded him to stay in Sicily. Another hagiographer noted that by the late sixth century the abbot John of Réomé had earned the respect of the most powerful people in Gaul, not least because he meditated on the *Instituta* and the *Collationes*—especially the books featuring Abba Isaac—and in the process kept his mind from getting distracted. And the *Rule of Benedict*, a Latin text that eventually became the most popular reference point for monastic discipline in Europe, presented Cassian's work as recommended reading and advised monks to listen to the *Collationes* after dinner and on fast days: these were times when the mind needed something energizing but not arousing.[7]

These are just a few of many examples. Cassian had many admiring readers, though his work, too, was controversial in some circles. His emphasis on lifelong disciplinary practices (behavioral, social, cognitive) as constitutive of an ethical life left its mark not only on monasticism but on Christianity more generally. That said, certain elements of Cassian's work never quite entered mainstream medieval psychology, and they might seem as surprising today as they did in the fifth century.[8]

ATTENTION IN THE COLLATIONES

One of the central preoccupations of the *Collationes* is the art of concentration. This art required many interlocking practices, and the diverse metaphors that Cassian and his interlocutors deploy reflect their sense of monastic practice as a multifaceted system of training. Distraction did not have a single solution. So like soldiers, monks disciplined themselves to respect chains of

command and group norms that could sustain them in combat. Like athletes, monks conditioned their bodies. Like artisans, monks honed skills that were essential to their craft—in their case, reading, memorizing, and above all monitoring the mind and heart. All these forms of training were necessary because a monk's spiritual growth depended on maintaining functional relationships between self and collective, mind and body, technique and reflection. Concentration on the divine wasn't going to happen simply by resolving to think harder, because a monk's mind was affected by the world in which it was embedded, by the fluctuating constraints of social networks, obligations, physical capacities, emotional states, knowledge, perceptions, and habits. Training across many domains was both ethically and psychologically necessary.

Practices that we recognize as the signature elements of Christian monasticism were, for Cassian, essential parts of that complex cognitive system. Renouncing property and family, joining

a community of likeminded practitioners, avoiding sex, eating sparingly: these were all strategies to minimize the things that didn't matter in order to stretch the mind out to God. But he also recommended forms of mental discipline that are accessible even to the nonmonks among us—think metacognitive habits, rather than major life changes—and this translation focuses on those. But for Cassian, they were only one part of the art of concentration.

He also insisted that attentiveness was not so much an achievement as a perpetual practice. Even the most expert monks got discouraged by distraction sometimes; the work was never over. But the highs could be exquisite—none more so, as far as Cassian was concerned, than what he called "fiery prayer." This was for him the consummate form of attention. A monk experiencing fiery prayer was not only locked on God. He was so absorbed in the experience, so overcome by spiritual sensation that the mind was incapable of dissecting the moment into something more

comprehensible and reductive. It was as close to an undistracted self as a monk could get.

But before diving into that deep form of attention, Cassian starts more straightforwardly. His guidebook (and this translation) begins with an orientation courtesy of the great Abba Moses, who tells Germanus and Cassian that, like everyone else who wants to acquire a skill, they will need short- and long-term goals. It's too easy to get distracted otherwise: without a destination to guide its movements, the mind will take endless detours without even realizing it's off course.

Cassian and Germanus know exactly what their ultimate goal is: the kingdom of God—both in the sense of salvation and also in the sense of an inner alignment with spiritual values in the present. But Moses has to help the friends identify the proximate goal that will help them get there, and that is clarity of heart, a state of being unmoved by disruptive tendencies within the self. With these goals, monks can map out

their way and refer to those plans to reorient themselves when they get lost.

After all, the mind can never completely avoid interruptions and distractions. What it *can* do is be selective with the thoughts it encounters or generates along the way—to go along with the ones that make sense for its goals, and to leave behind the ones that don't. We can't stop our minds from moving around, but we can give them better or worse things to think about.

But even with a map in mind, monks still struggled. The selection from book 7 of the *Collationes* speaks to their frustrations. Cassian and Germanus vent to Abba Serenus: after all the time they've spent as monks in the desert, the only thing they seem to have acquired is a deeper awareness of their own inability to concentrate. When they feel themselves advancing toward their destinations, their minds are led off course by innumerable daily distractions—only to suddenly return to what they were supposed to be thinking about, then wander away again. Serenus

cuts off their complaining when Germanus suggests that concentration has nothing to do with self-control. It's natural for the mind to move around, Serenus grants, but where it goes and what it thinks about is up to us. Germanus and Cassian need more training.

In books 9 and 10, which are sometimes considered to be the culmination of the *Collationes*, Germanus and Cassian learn from Abba Isaac how to reach a state of total concentration—and more specifically, concentration in prayer, because as Isaac points out, sometimes we concentrate on things we shouldn't.[9]

Although there are infinite permutations of prayer, depending on who is praying and what their mind is like in the moment, the monks are especially keen to experience fiery prayer, that state of losing touch with the outside world while the mind becomes illuminated and pours out thoughts in a powerful flow. (Although the modern concept of flow was coined by the psychologist Mihaly Csikszentmihalyi, the

metaphor of flow to describe attentive and absorptive thinking recurs throughout Cassian's book.)[10] According to Isaac, what makes this state of mind possible is a sense of genuine feeling for the subject at hand, rather than a superficial commitment to it. Almost anything can catalyze this feeling, but it can't be faked, and in all cases the necessary precondition is a calm and clear heart.

But Germanus and Cassian aren't satisfied with this general advice. They want a particular method that they can reliably follow, to experience that absorptive concentration instead of constantly getting waylaid by distraction and struggling to refocus. Isaac suggests that they memorize a single line of text, a psalm verse that asks for God's help, and to intone it as a kind of mantra or mnemonic throughout the day—not only as they settle down to meditate but *all the time*. The mantra would serve as a regular dosage of sage advice, to remind them of their priorities and goals. It would also be a constant companion,

something to turn to in monks' many moments of weakness. But for Germanus this advice is still not enough. The problem is getting circular. "How do we hold onto that verse?"

Abba Nesteros takes a different tack. He tells the pair to read and recite their sacred texts all the time, which should not only keep their minds busy but also saturate and transform them with images that will flush out unwanted thoughts and useless memories, even the stories and songs they learned as kids. You can't just clean out your mind and leave it blank, Nesteros says. You've got to replace all those vivid images and ideas with other things to work with. Imagine your mind as a cool, calm sanctuary that will give you access to God. Store that vault with things you treasure, and eventually it will overflow with thoughts you actually want to be thinking.

In the last two books of the *Collationes* the abbas Theonas and Abraham offer some final words of encouragement and warning to

Germanus and Cassian, who are still fighting to stay focused. Nobody can experience the divine all the time, Theonas assures them. The mind is bound to slip and fall. But you need to take the challenge seriously. Think of yourself as a tightrope walker, with the line stretched tight between yourselves and God. You need to be afraid of falling: *this* will help you take your concentration seriously!

Germanus suggests to Abraham that maybe the best way to concentrate is to move back home. It would be easier to avoid distractions if he didn't have to think about supporting himself and if he weren't always getting so many visitors. Not a chance, says Abraham. The idea that you can escape to somewhere even more remote, or even more peaceful, is an empty fantasy. There will always be people to distract us, responsibilities to keep us busy, and opportunities to make us second-guess the choices we already made. Rather than give up on a life that generations of monks had already engineered to

help themselves concentrate, they should treat small interruptions or challenges as beneficial breaks. Otherwise even the most focused minds will falter.

There is a great gulf between our age and the world of late antiquity. But Cassian was part of an enthusiastic and analytical subculture that speaks to struggles we share in common. Like early Christian monks, we are still easily distracted—and we keep wishing we weren't. Sixteen hundred years later, their conversations still have things to teach us. And when Cassian and his interlocutors speak, they are simultaneously stern and empathetic, out of a conviction that it's possible to make the mind stronger, but impossible to control it completely.

NOTES ON THE TRANSLATION

In its full form, the *Collationes* consists of twenty-four consultations and around 150,000 words. The excerpts here are drawn from seven consultations and represent less than 10 percent of the whole—so this translation conveys only a fraction of what Cassian shared with his readers.[11] But it operates in an undeniably premodern mode: compiling excerpts of treasured texts into abridgements or anthologies was common practice in late antique and medieval book culture. It was a way of drawing on the knowledge and traditions of prior generations while shifting it, like the twist of a kaleidoscope, into something different. Through curation and recombination, the old became new, offering insights that spoke to the questions and preoccupations of different audiences. Cassian's work certainly

received this treatment. Compilers set to abridging and excerpting the *Collationes* not long after Cassian had finished it, and even its enthusiastic monastic readers drew from it choosily. For instance, the abbot Eugippius of Castellum Lucullanum (outside of Naples) drew up a monastic rule in the sixth century that included two snippets of the *Collationes*, both of which emphasized the importance of keeping the mind attentive for the sake of screening sexual thoughts before they made a monk aroused. So although my selective use of Cassian speaks to contemporary interests, it's also an extension of textual practices that are well over a millennium old.[12]

This translation counterbalances the modern and premodern in an even more basic way, in its effort to bridge fifth-century Latin and twenty-first-century American English. Cassian and the Christian monks of late antique Egypt developed a cognitive culture that is both relatable and foreign to us today. I wanted this translation

to welcome readers into that world, to make it intelligible and to showcase its shrewd analyses of how minds work.[13] That meant loosening up the English in a way that highlights the earnestness and tenacity of Cassian's speakers, rather than replicating the sinuous and nested qualities of his very distinctive Latin and in the process making them sound stilted. At the same time, I also wanted to allow the monks to remain a bit strange—partly because they were quite self-consciously countercultural in their time, and also because their distinctly late antique attitudes can't be fully assimilated into ours.[14]

Cassian himself knew that translations were both insufficient and illuminating. In his consultations with Abba Moses and Abba Isaac, he notes subtle differences between biblical passages as they're rendered in Greek versus Latin: the comparison results in a sharper understanding of issues that the Latin on its own does not quite convey.[15] But this doesn't lead Cassian to conclude that translation is too misleading to be

worth the undertaking. After all, the entire project of his *Collationes* relies on translation. The Egyptian elders whom Germanus and Cassian consulted mostly spoke in Coptic, through a Greek translator for the benefit of their guests; and then Cassian sculpted these sessions into Latin, the native language of his audiences in southern Gaul.[16]

A final point about my translation. When it comes to certain key terms in Cassian's work, I've veered away from lexical choices that are common in English translations but which tend to distort our sense of the late antique text. The usual rendering for *vitium*, for example, is "vice"—a word that has acquired centuries of doctrinal associations that weren't in play when Cassian was writing. He meant something more like "weakness" or "vulnerability." Likewise *virtus* is flattened by the English "virtue," because Cassian uses the term to convey the mix of masculinity, strength, and fitness that could help monks stay fixed on their goals. *Passio* is often

translated as "passion," but the word has its own dogmatic pedigree that effectively downplays the roiling reactions that Cassian was trying to understand and control.[17] *Discretio* was not so much "discretion" (in our sense of tact) as it was a technical term for the detective work that monks were supposed to perform on their own thoughts—to determine which ones were good and which ones were dangerous distractions. And *puritas cordis*, usually expressed in English as "purity of heart," is rendered here as "clarity" or "tranquility of heart" to underscore the psychological slant of Cassian's spirituality. The term was his spin on the concept of *apatheia*, or freedom from emotional investments and reactionism: this was originally a Stoic ethic that Cassian's teacher Evagrius had made central to monastic practice. But *apatheia* had become controversial by the time Cassian was writing, and some critics contended that to promote it was to imply that it was possible to control the self without any help from God. So Cassian proposed

the heart as a kind of passageway: when the heart was clear and calm and stable, it amounted to an act of complete commitment or love that enabled the mind to stretch out to the divine.[18] These are just a few of the most obvious examples where traditional translations tame the force of the original. The *Collationes* is an exploratory and experimental text, and I've tried to capture its sense of inquiry here.

HOW TO FOCUS

[1.1] Cum in heremo Sciti, ubi monachorum probatissimi patres et omnis commorabatur perfectio, abbatem Moysen, qui inter illos egregios flores suauius non solum actuali, uerum etiam theoretica uirtute fragrabat, institutione eius fundari cupiens expetissem una cum sancto abbate Germano (cum quo mihi ab ipso tirocinio ac rudimentis militiae spiritalis ita indiuiduum deinceps contubernium tam in coenobio quam in heremo fuit, ut cuncti ad significandam sodalitatis ac propositi nostri parilitatem pronuntiarent unam mentem atque animam duobus inesse corporibus),

GOALS

Cassian and Germanus Consult
Abba Moses of Scetis

The desert of Scetis: home to the most battle-tested monastic elders and their many perfect achievements. Abba Moses was the sweetest of all those extraordinary flowers there; his practical and also his contemplative powers were full of fragrance. I wanted to get some grounding in his teaching, so the holy abba Germanus and I *had* to seek him out. Germanus had been with me ever since we had entered the spiritual military and started basic training, and from then on, we were such inseparable bunkmates in both the monastic community and the desert that everyone remarked on the equality of our companionship and our sense of purpose. They said that we were one mind and soul in two bodies.

pariterque ab eodem abbate aedificationis ser-
monem fusis lacrimis posceremus (quippe cuius
hunc animi rigorem manifestissime noueramus, ut
nisi fideliter desiderantibus et cum omni cordis
contritione quaerentibus nequaquam adquiesceret
ianuam perfectionis aperire, ne scilicet, si passim
uel nolentibus eam uel tepide sitientibus exhiberet,
res necessarias et quae solis perfectionem cupienti-
bus debent esse conpertae, indignis et fastidiose
suscipientibus pandens aut iactantiae uitium aut
proditionis crimen uideretur incurrere), tandem
fatigatus precibus nostris ita exorsus est.

[1.2.1] Omnes, inquit, artes ac disciplinae scopon quendam, id est destinationem, et telos, hoc
est finem proprium habent, ad quem respiciens
uniuscuiusque artis industrius adpetitor cunctos
labores et pericula atque dispendia aequanimiter
libenterque sustentat.

And now both of us were pouring out tears[19] and begging Abba Moses to edify us with his words. (We did this because we knew he was so notoriously strict that he'd agree to open the door of perfection only to people who longed for it in good faith and sought it out in a state of total anguish. He didn't want to seem to be committing the crime of betrayal or giving into the impulse to show off. Revealing that door indiscriminately to people who weren't up for it, or who were only sort of interested, would result in the disclosure of vital matters—things that only people seeking perfection should learn—to unworthy recipients who wouldn't know what it all was worth.) Eventually he was worn down by our pleas and began to speak.

"Every acquired skill and every discipline," he said, "has a *scopos* and a *telos*, some immediate goal and some ultimate goal that is particular to it. Practitioners of any skilled craft will gladly and good-naturedly work through all

nam et agricola nunc torridos solis radios,
nunc pruinas et glaciem non declinans terram
infatigabiliter scindit et indomitas agri glaebas
frequenti subigit uomere, dum scopon seruat,
ut eam cunctis sentibus expurgatam uniuersisque
graminibus absolutam in modum solubilis hare-
nae exercendo comminuat, finem, id est perceptionem copiosarum frugum et exuberantiam
segetum non alias adepturum se esse confidens,
quo uel ipse deinceps uitam securus exigere uel
suam possit amplificare substantiam. [1.2.2]
referta etiam frugibus horrea libenter exhaurit
easque putribus sulcis instanti labore commen-
dat, praesentem deminutionem futurarum mes-
sium contemplatione non sentiens.

illi etiam, qui negotiationum solent exercere
commercia, non incertos pelagi timent casus, non
ulla discrimina perhorrescunt, dum ad finem
quaestus spe praepeti prouocantur.

nec non etiam hi qui militiae mundialis ambitione flammantur, dum prospiciunt honorum
ac potentiae finem, peregrinationum exitia ac

their fatigue and risks and costs as they keep those goals in mind.[20]

"Take a farmer, for instance, who tirelessly breaks up the soil and plows through the untilled clods of his field over and over again, without giving up in the frost and ice or in the withering rays of the sun. He does this while keeping his eye on his immediate goal of clearing away all the thorns, purging all the vegetation, and crumbling the earth into a loamy texture. He is certain that this is the only way he'll achieve his ultimate goal: a yield of copious produce and abundant grain that will enable him to live comfortably or even to build up his wealth. He's even willing to draw down the produce from his storehouses when supplies are already getting low, and he works hard to entrust their seeds to the fallow farrows. He doesn't see it as a shortage in the present, because he is focused on future harvests.

"Likewise the merchants who work in wholesale trade aren't afraid of what might

pericula non sentiunt nec praesentibus aerumnis bellisque frangunter, dum propositum sibi dignitatis finem cupiunt obtinere.

[1.2.3] habet ergo et nostra professio scopon proprium ac finem suum, pro quo labores cunctos non solum infatigabiliter, uerum etiam gratanter inpendimus, ob quem nos ieiuniorum inedia non fatigat, uigiliarum lassitudo delectat, lectio ac meditatio scripturarum continuata non satiat, labor etiam incessabilis nuditasque et omnium rerum priuatio, horror quoque huius uastissimae solitudinis non deterret. ob quem uos ipsi procul dubio parentum spreuistis affectum

happen unexpectedly on the open sea. As long as the drive to profit propels them to an ultimate goal, there isn't any hazard that scares them.

Not even the members of the earthly military who are stoked by ambition notice the ravages or dangers of their campaigns when they have the ultimate goal of honors and influence to look forward to. And they aren't shattered by losses or battles in the moment, as long as they're eagerly anticipating the ultimate goal of the promotion they've visualized for themselves.

"Our own profession has particular immediate and ultimate goals, too, and we devote all our labors tirelessly and even enthusiastically to them. This is why fasting doesn't wear us out, why the fatigue from keeping vigil all night appeals to us, why constant reading and meditating on the scriptures is never enough for us, and why incessant work and nakedness and complete dispossession and this chilling expanse of solitude doesn't scare us off. And it is

et patrium solum ac delicias mundi tot pertran-
sitis regionibus despexistis, ut ad nos homines
rusticos et idiotas atque in hoc heremi squalore
degentes peruenire possetis. propter quod re-
spondete, inquit, mihi quae sit destinatio uestra
uel finis, qui ad haec omnia libentissime sus-
tinenda uos prouocat.

[1.3] Et cum persisteret nostram elicere super
hac interrogatione sententiam, respondimus
regni caelorum causa haec cuncta tolerari.

[1.4.1] Ad quod ille: Bene, inquit: argute de
fine dixistis. qui uero debeat esse scopos noster, id est destinatio, cui iugiter inhaerentes
finem ualeamus adtingere, prae omnibus nosse
debetis.
et cum ignorationem confessi simpliciter fuis-
semus, adiecit: in omni ut dixi arte ac disciplina
praecedit quidam scopos, id est animae destinatio siue incessabilis mentis intentio. quam

undoubtedly why you yourselves rejected the affection of your families and turned away from your only homeland and from the delightful things in the world, traveling long distances so that you could visit us of all people—rednecks and hicks living in this desolate desert. So tell me: what are your immediate and ultimate goals? What's compelling you two to endure all of this so willingly?"

Since Moses kept trying to elicit a response from us, we answered that the kingdom of the heavens was the reason to endure all these things.

He replied, "Nicely done! You've given an incisive answer about your ultimate goal. But before anything else, you should really know what our scopos should be. I'm talking about our immediate goal, the thing we stick to all the time so that we're eventually able to reach the ultimate goal."

We openly admitted that we didn't know. So he went on: "Like I said, there is a particular scopos

nisi quis omni studio perseuerantiaque seruau-
erit, nec ad finem desiderati fructus poterit
peruenire.

[1.4.2] nam ut dixi agricola finem habens secure
copioseque uiuendi in prouentu segctum fe-
cundarum scopon, id est destinationem gerit
agrum suum cunctis sentibus expurgare eumque
uniuersis infructuosis uacuare graminibus, nec aliter se quieti finis opulentiam adepturum esse con-
fidit, nisi id, quod usu obtinere desiderat, quadam
prius operis ac spei suae ratione possideat.

negotiator quoque conparandarum mercium
desiderium non deponit, per quod possit quaes-
tuosius diuitias congregare, quia frustra concu-
pisceret lucrum, nisi uiam qua ad id tenderet
elegisset.

that leads the way in every single skill and discipline. Think of it as an immediate goal for the soul, or a relentless mental attentiveness. If you don't focus on it with all your effort and perseverance, you won't be able to reach your ultimate goal and enjoy the payoff you've been waiting for.

"For instance, as I said before, the farmer whose ultimate goal is to live comfortably and prosperously off his plentiful yields of grain operates with the scopos or immediate goal of clearing all the thorns from his field and getting rid of all the weeds. He doesn't assume that he'll achieve his ultimate goal—getting rich—by doing nothing; he knows for certain that he'll possess what he really wants to have only by means of his plan of hard work and hope.

"The same is true of the merchant. He never gives up the drive to procure merchandise, which is such a lucrative way for him to accumulate wealth. It would be pointless for him to pursue profit without deciding how to get there.

et qui certis quibusque dignitatibus mundi huius cupiunt honorari, cui se officio uel ordini debeant mancipare ante proponunt, ut per legitimum spei tramitem finem quoque ualeant desideratae dignitatis adtingere.

[1.4.3] itaque et uiae nostrae finis quidem est regnum dei. quid ucro sit scopos debet diligenter inquiri: qui si nobis similiter conpertus non fuerit, frustra nitendo fatigabimur, quia sine uia tendentibus labor est itineris, non profectus.

ad quod obstupescentibus nobis senex intulit: finis quidem nostrae professionis ut diximus regnum dei seu regnum caelorum est, destinatio uero, id est scopos, puritas cordis, sine qua ad illum finem inpossibile est quempiam peruenire.

"As for people who want to be honored with some particular distinction the world has to offer: the first thing they do is decide what job or office to land on, so that by setting their hopes on the right course of action, they can arrive at their ultimate goal of the accolade they've always wanted.

"In the same way, when it comes to our own path, the end point is the kingdom of God. But as for what our scopos might be, we should really make a careful investigation. If we don't figure it out like other people do, we'll wear ourselves out to the point of exhaustion—all for nothing, because if we don't follow a path, our work is a journey that goes nowhere."

As we sat in astonishment at what he'd said, the old man made this proposition: "As we said, the ultimate goal that is specific to our profession is the kingdom of God, the kingdom of the heavens. And in fact our immediate goal, our scopos, is clarity and tranquility of the heart.[21]

[1.4.4] in hac ergo destinatione defigentes nostrae directionis obtutus uelut ad certam lineam
cursum rectissimum dirigemus, ac si paululum
quid ab hac cogitatio nostra deflexerit, ad contemplationem eius ilico recurrentes rursus eam
uelut ad quandam normam rectissime corrige-
mus, quae semper omnes conatus nostros ad
unum hoc reuocans signum arguet statim, si a
proposita directione mens nostra uel paululum
deuiauerit.

[1.5.1] Quemadmodum hi, quibus usus est
bellica tela tractandi, cum ante regem mundi
huius artis suae cupiunt peritiam demonstrare, in
paruissima quaedam scutula, quae depicta in se
continent praemia, iacula uel sagittas intorquere
contendunt, certi quod non alias nisi destinationis suae linea ad finem possint desiderati praemii
peruenire, quo tum demum utique potientur,
cum propositum scopon ualuerint obtinere:

Without that clarity, it's totally impossible to reach the ultimate goal.

"So we should fix our navigation on this immediate goal, like we're steering ourselves along a set line down a very straight route. And even if our thinking were to veer away from it a bit, we would hurry to set it in our sights again, like making a precise correction with a ruler—a ruler that keeps drawing all our ventures back to this one guideline and alerting us immediately if our mind takes even a little detour from the course in front of us.

"Take, for example, people who are trained in handling military projectiles. When they want to showcase their expertise in this skill in the presence of a king in some part of the world, they shoot their javelins or arrows at miniscule targets that have prizes depicted on them. They're sure that the only way to obtain the ultimate goal of the prize they're after is to follow the sightline of their immediate goal. And

qui si forte ab eorum fuerit subtractus intuitu, quantumlibet a recto tramite cassa imperi-
torum deerret intentio, excidisse se tamen ab
illius disciplinatae lineae directione non sen-
tient, quia nullum habent certum signum quod
uel peritiam directionis probet uel arguat praui-
tatem. et ideo cum inutiles in aëra uacuumque
fuderint iactus, in quo peccauerint quoue de
cepti sint diiudicare non possunt, quippe quos
nullum accusat indicium quantum a directione
discesserint, nec quo deinceps corrigere uel reuocare debeant lineam disciplinae docere potest
passiuus obtutus.

[1.5.2] ita igitur et nostri propositi finis quidem secundum apostolum uita aeterna est, ita
eodem pronuntiante: habentes quidem fructum
uestrum in sanctificationem, finem uero uitam
aeternam, scopos uero est puritas cordis, quam
sanctificationem non inmerito nuncupauit, sine

then in the end, they *do* get that ultimate goal, when they to stick to their set scopos.

"But if the target happened to be taken away, nobody—not even an inexperienced shooter who aimed way off the right trajectory—would know whether they'd deviated from the designated line, because they wouldn't have any indicator to tell whether their aim was true or crooked. And the result of having dumped their useless shots into the open air would be that they couldn't tell where they went wrong or where they were misled, obviously because there wouldn't be any telltale sign of how far they'd gone off course. If your eye doesn't know where to look, it can't offer any guidance about where to adjust or realign your aim.

"So as I was saying, the ultimate goal that has been set before us is everlasting life, as the apostle Paul declared: 'Ye have your fruit unto holiness, and the end everlasting life.' The scopos here is clarity of heart, and the word he used for it was 'holiness,' with good reason.

qua praedictus finis non poterit adprehendi, acsi
dixisset aliis uerbis: habentes quidem scopon
uestrum in cordis puritate, finem uero uitam aeternam. de qua destinatione docens nos idem
beatus apostolus ipsum nomen, id est scopon,
significanter expressit ita dicens: quae posteriora sunt obliuiscens, ad ea uero quae in ante sunt
extendens me, ad destinatum persequor, ad
brauium supernae uocationis domini.

[1.5.3] quod euidentius in Graeco ponitur
κατὰ σκοπὸν διώκω, id est secundum destinationem persequor, tamquam si dixisset: hac destinatione qua illa quae posteriora sunt obliuiscor,
id est anterioris hominis uitia, ad finem brauii
caelestis peruenire contendo.

quidquid ergo nos ad hunc scopon, id est
puritatem cordis potest dirigere, tota uirtute
sectandum est, quidquid autem ab hac retrahit,
ut perniciosum ac noxium deuitandum. pro hac
enim uniuersa agimus atque toleramus, pro hac
parentes, patria, dignitates, diuitiae, deliciae

Without clarity of heart, the ultimate goal he mentioned would be unattainable. It was as if he'd said in so many words 'Ye have your scopos unto clarity of heart, and the end everlasting life.' And the same blessed apostle literally used the word scopos in teaching us about this immediate goal. He said: 'Forgetting those things which are behind, and reaching forth unto those things which are before, I press toward the goal for the prize of the high calling of the Lord.'

"The connection is more obvious in the Greek original: 'I press toward the immediate goal' is *kata skopon diōkō*. It's as if he'd said, 'with this immediate goal I forget the things behind me—the weaknesses of the person I was before—and I go after the ultimate goal of the celestial prize.'[22]

"And so whatever can point us toward this immediate goal of clarity and tranquility of heart should be followed with all our might, and whatever drags us away from it should be treated as a destructive and toxic thing. Everything we

mundi huius et uoluptas uniuersa contemnitur, ut scilicet puritas cordis perpetua retentetur.

[1.5.4] hac itaque nobis destinatione proposita semper actus nostri et cogitationes ad eam obtinendam rectissime dirigentur. quae si prae oculis nostris iugiter statuta non fuerit, non solum cunctos labores nostros uacuos pariter atque instabiles reddens in cassum eos ac sine ullo emolumento conpellet effundi,

sed etiam cogitationes omnes diuersas sibique contrarias suscitabit. necesse est enim mentem quo recurrat cuiue principaliter inhaereat non habentem per singulas horas atque momenta pro incursuum uarietate mutari atque ex his quae extrinsecus accedunt in illum statum continuo transformari qui sibi primus occurrerit.

[1.6.1] Hinc namque est quod nonnullos mundi huius maximas facultates et non solum

pursue and put up with, we do for the sake of this scopos. For its sake we disregard families, homelands, professional advancements, wealth, the world's charms, really every single pleasurable thing: all to maintain a clear heart always.

"And once this immediate goal is in front of us, our actions and thoughts should always be steered along the straightest path toward achieving it. If it isn't constantly propped up in front of our eyes, it would make all our efforts hollow and flimsy. It would be a waste—all that to no end, with no payoff.

"It would also stir up all sorts of conflicting thoughts. When the mind doesn't have a head-quarters to return to and to keep in close contact with, it will inevitably get bounced around by all sorts of distractions, and it will just keep taking on the shape of whatever external stimulus it comes across next.

"We have seen this at play among people who don't put any stock in pricey assets—whether

multa auri atque argenti talenta, uerum etiam
praediorum magnificentiam contemnentes post
haec uidimus pro scalpello, pro graphio, pro acu,
pro calamo commoueri. qui si contemplationem
cordis mundi fixam tenerent, numquam utique
pro paruis rebus admitterent, quod ne pro mag-
nis ac pretiosis incurrerent opibus, easdem penitus abicere maluerunt.

[1.6.2] nam et plerumque nonnulli tanto zelo
codicem seruant, ut eum ne leuiter quidem legi
uel contingi ab aliquo sinant, et inde occasiones
inpatientiae ac mortis incurrunt, unde monen-
tur stipendia patientiae et caritatis adquirere,
cumque omnes diuitias suas pro Christi amore
disperserint, pristinum tamen cordis affectum
in rebus minimis retentantes et pro ipsis nonnumquam mobiliter irascentes, ueluti qui non
habeant apostolicam caritatem, ex omnibus
infructuosi sterilesque redduntur. quod in
spiritu beatus apostolus praeuidens et si dis-
tribuero, inquit, in cibos pauperum omnes
facultates meas et tradidero corpus meum ut

it's piles of cash in gold and silver, or even luxe estates—only to be shaken up about a knife, a stylus, a needle, a pen.[23] But if they were keeping their heart's concentration tidy, there's no way they would let small things clutter it up, given that they'd already decided to get rid of their sizeable and valuable holdings so as not to run into the same problem!

"It's often the case, for instance, that some people will guard a book so jealously that they can barely stand to let someone else read or even touch it. In the process, they turn opportunities to reap the rewards of being accommodating and charitable into opportunities to reap the rewards of intolerance and death. Although they've distributed all their wealth out of love for Christ, they still hold onto their heart's old proclivity for the most insignificant things, and they can rapidly fly into a rage over them, just like those people who do not have apostolic charity and are rendered unproductive and sterile. The blessed

ardeam, caritatem autem non habuero, nihil mihi prodest.

[1.6.3] unde liquido conprobatur perfectionem non statim nuditate nec priuatione omnium facultatum seu dignitatum abiectione contingi, nisi fuerit caritas illa cuius apostolus membra describit, quae in sola cordis puritate consistit. nam quid est aliud non aemulari, non inflari, non inritari, non agere perperam, non quaerere quae sua sunt, non super iniquitate gaudere, non cogitare malum et reliqua, nisi cor perfectum atque mundissimum deo semper offerre et intactum a cunctis perturbationibus custodire?

[1.7.1] Omnia igitur huius gratia gerenda adpetendaque sunt nobis. pro hac solitudo

apostle foresaw this in his spirit and said that 'if I should distribute all my goods to feed the poor, and if I should deliver my body to be burned, and have not charity, it profiteth me nothing.'

"Clearly this proves that perfection can't be attained the instant you strip yourself down, or deprive yourself of all your properties, or jettison your titles—unless you have that charity whose component parts the apostle described, this love that can be found only in the clarity and tranquility of the heart. After all, what does it mean to *not* be competitive, not be pompous, not be irritated, not be misleading, not misbehave, not be self-serving, not take pleasure in things that are wrong, not think about evil, and all the rest? What does it mean except to offer a refined and spotlessly clean heart to God always, and to keep it away from any and all psychological turbulence?

"And so everything we do and strive for should be done for the sake of clarity of

sectanda est, pro hac ieiunia, uigilias, labores,
corporis nuditatem, lectionem ceterasque uirtutes debere nos suscipere nouerimus, ut scilicet
per illas ab uniuersis passionibus noxiis inlaesum parare cor nostrum et conseruare possimus
et ad perfectionem caritatis istis gradibus inni-
tendo conscendere, et non propter has obseru-
antias, si forte honesta ac necessaria occupatione
praeuenti sollemnitatem districtionis nostrae non
potuerimus implere, incidamus in tristitiam uel
iram siue indignationem, ob quae expugnanda
illud quod praetermissum est fueramus acturi.

[1.7.2] non enim tantum est lucrum ieiunii
quantum irae dispendium nec tantus lectione capitur fructus quantum contemptu fratris incur-
ritur detrimentum. ea igitur quae sequentia sunt,
id est ieiunia, uigiliae, anachoresis, meditatio
scripturarum, propter principalem scopon, id est
puritatem cordis, quod est caritas, nos conuenit
exercere et non propter illa principalem hanc
proturbare uirtutem, qua in nobis integra in-
laesaque durante nihil oberit, si aliquid eorum

heart. Solitude should be pursued for it. We know that we should take on fasts, vigils, manual labor, nakedness, reading, and other feats for it—so that we can condition our heart and keep it unharmed from all those toxic pathologies,[24] climbing those steps to a perfect state of love. And if some legitimate and pressing task happens to come up and we can't carry out our usual strict regimen, we shouldn't get sad or angry or annoyed. The very point of our regimen is to overcome such disturbances!

"After all, the advantages of fasting don't make up for the loss incurred when we're angry, and the benefits of reading don't make up for the damage done when we despise a brother. We're supposed to practice this series of exercises—fasts, vigils, isolation, meditating on the scriptures—for the sake of the fundamental scopos, for the sake of clarity of heart, which is love. We shouldn't counteract this fundamental source of strength in us simply for the sake of

quae sequentia sunt pro necessitate fuerit praetermissum: siquidem nec proderit uniuersa fe-
cisse adempta hac qua diximus principali causa,
cuius obtentu sunt omnia peragenda.

[1.7.3] ob hoc enim quis ferramenta cuiuslibet artis instituere sibimet ac praeparare festi-
nat, non ut ea possideat otiosa nec ut emolumenti
illius fructum qui speratur ex ipsis in nuda in-
strumentorum possessione constituat, sed ut
eorum ministerio peritiam finemque illius disciplinae cuius haec adiumenta sunt efficaciter
adprehendat. igitur ieiunia, uigiliae, meditatio
scripturarum, nuditas ac priuatio omnium facultatum non perfectio, sed perfectionis instrumenta sunt, quia non in ipsis consistit disciplinae illius finis, sed per illa peruenitur ad finem.

[1.7.4] in cassum igitur haec exercitia molietur, quisque his uelut summo bono contentus

our exercises. If something in the series has to be skipped, nothing will harm us as long as that power remains intact and unharmed. It won't do us any good if we perform the entire sequence while having abandoned what we've said is the fundamental reason to accomplish anything.

"This is why people work quickly to set up and outfit themselves with the tools of whatever their trade is: the point isn't to get their hands on some knick-knacks, or to lay claim to the bare value that the equipment itself might be worth, but to use them to gain expertise and attain the ultimate goal of the discipline they were designed for. So you see, fasts, vigils, meditating on the scriptures, nakedness, and total dispossession don't amount to a state of perfection. They are only the tools of perfection, because the ultimate goal of our discipline doesn't reside in them; it is reached *through* them.

"It's useless to undertake these exercises if you're satisfied with fixing your heart's attention

intentionem sui cordis huc usque defixerit et non ad capiendum finem, propter quem haec adpetenda sunt, omne studium uirtutis extenderit, habens quidem disciplinae illius instrumenta, finem uero, in quo omnis fructus consistit, ignorans. quidquid igitur potest istam mentis nostrae puritatem tranquillitatemque turbare, quamuis utile ac necessarium uideatur, ut noxium deuitandum est. hac enim norma et errorum peruagationumque omnium dispersiones poterimus euadere et desideratum finem linea certae directionis adtingere.

[1.16] GERMANVS: Quid ergo est quod etiam nolentibus, immo uero etiam nescientibus nobis ita superfluae cogitationes subtiliter ac latenter inrepunt, ut non solum eas expellere, uerum etiam intellegere ac deprehendere difficultatis

on them alone, as if they were the greatest good, rather than on achieving your ultimate goal—which is the whole reason to strive to do these exercises. Even with the tools of the discipline in your hands you'll have expended all your effort and strength without knowing what the ultimate goal really is. Everything that is profitable is related to that goal. So anything that is capable of disturbing that clarity and calm of our mind, no matter how useful or essential it seems, should be treated as toxic. This is the ruler that will enable us to correct course from all our missteps and distractions, and to reach our desired goal along its clear straight line."

Later in the Conversation with Moses

Germanus asked, "Why is it that—even when we don't want it to happen—useless thoughts break in sneakily and secretly, without us even knowing, making it beyond difficult to notice and catch them, let alone kick them out? I mean,

inmodicae sit? potest ergo mens aliquando ab istis uacua repperiri et numquam huiuscemodi inlusionibus incursari?

[1.17.1] MOYSES: Mentem quidem non interpellari cogitationibus inpossibile est, suscipere uero eas siue respuere omni studenti possibile est. quemadmodum igitur ortus earum non omnimodis pendet a nobis, ita reprobatio uel electio consistit in nobis. nec tamen ex eo quod diximus inpossibile esse mentem cogitationibus non adiri, totum uel incursui uel illis spiritibus tribuendum est qui eas nobis nituntur ingerere. alioquin nec liberum in homine maneret arbitrium nec in nobis staret nostrae correctionis industria.

[1.17.2] sed est, inquam, nostrum magna ex parte, ut cogitationum qualitas emendetur et uel sanctae ac spiritales in cordibus nostris uel terrenae carnalesque concrescant. ideo namque frequens lectio et iugis adhibetur meditatio scripturarum, ut exinde nobis spiritalis memoriae

can the mind ever be free of such thoughts? Is it always going to be the target of scams like this?"

Moses said: "It's truly impossible for the mind not to be interrupted by thoughts. But it *is* possible, for anyone who makes the effort, to welcome them in or kick them out. Their origin doesn't have everything to do with us, but it's up to us to reject or accept them. And yet, despite what we've said about the impossibility of the mind not being attacked by thoughts, we shouldn't chalk everything up to assault and to the spirits who are trying to inflict these thoughts on us. That wouldn't leave any room for the human will to be free, and we'd lose the drive to improve ourselves.[25]

"Instead I would say that it's mainly through our doing that the nature of our thoughts can be improved and take shape—either as sacred and spiritual thoughts or as earthly and material ones. This is precisely the reason we take the time to read regularly and to meditate on the

praebeatur occasio, idcirco decantatio crebra psalmorum, ut adsidua nobis exinde conpunctio ministretur, idcirco uigiliarum ac ieiuniorum orationumque sedulitas adhibetur, ut extenuata mens non terrena sapiat, sed caelestia contempletur. quibus rursum neglegentia inrepente cessantibus necesse est ut mens uitiorum squalore concreta in carnalem partem mox inclinetur et conruat.

[1.18.1] Quod exercitium cordis non incongrue molarum similitudini conparatur, quas meatus aquarum praeceps impetu rotante prouoluit. quae nullatenus quidem cessare possunt ab opere suo aquarum inpulsibus circumactae: in eius uero qui praeest situm est potestate, utrumnam triticum malit an hordeum loliumue comminui. illud quippe est procul dubio conmolendum,

scriptures constantly: to create opportunities to furnish our memory with something spiritual. The reason we chant the psalms one after the other is so that the piercing pain of the conscience can be at hand to help us. And the reason we take the time to carry out vigils and fasts and prayers is so that our mind is expanded and gazes on celestial things rather than savoring what's on earth. Conversely, when neglect creeps in and we stop doing these exercises, the mind will inevitably get stuck in the muck of its flaws, and it won't be long before it turns to physical concerns, and collapses.

"So it's fitting that the functioning of the heart is thought to closely resemble the workings of a millstone, which is set spinning when the rush of water propels the mechanism to rotate. There's no way for the millstone to stop running as long as the water pressure is wheeling it around. But what the overseer can control is the choice of what to grind: wheat or barley

quod ingestum ab illo fuerit cui operis illius cura commissa est.

[1.18.2] ita igitur etiam mens per uitae praesentis incursus undique ingruentibus temptationum torrentibus circumacta uacua quidem cogitationum aestibus esse non poterit: quales uero uel amittere uel parare sibi debeat, studii ac diligentiae suae prouidebit industria. si enim ut diximus ad sanctarum scripturarum meditationem iugiter recurramus ac memoriam nostram ad recordationem spiritalium rerum et desiderium perfectionis spemque futurae beatitudinis erigamus, necesse est ut ortae cogitationes exinde spiritales in his quae meditati sumus mentem faciant inmorari.

[1.18.3] sin uero desidia seu neglegentia superati uitiis et otiosis confabulationibus occupemur seu curis mundanis et superfluis sollicitudinibus inplicemur, consequenter exinde uelut quaedam zizaniorum species generata operationem quoque

or the dreaded darnel.[26] This much is patently obvious: it has to mill whatever its operator pours into it.

"The mind is like that, too: it just can't be free from the flux of thoughts while it's wheeled around through the currents of the present life by the violent rapids rushing all around it. But through intentional and careful effort, it will determine what kind of materials it should throw out or process for its own use. As I've said, if we repeatedly meditate on the sacred scriptures; and if we elevate our memory to the recollection of spiritual subjects, a longing for perfection, and the hope of the ultimate bliss to come—then the spiritual thoughts that spring from our meditations will naturally keep our mind occupied.

"But if we're overcome by laziness or neglect and get caught up in bad habits and pointless chitchat, or if we become entangled in mundane preoccupations and unnecessary concerns, it would be like supplying our mechanism with

nostro cordi noxiam ministrabit, et secundum sententiam domini saluatoris ubi fuerit thesaurus operum seu intentionis nostrae, ibi et cor nostrum necessario permanebit.

some kind of weed that is toxic to our heart. For according to the saying of the Lord Savior, where the treasure of our deeds or attention is, there will our heart necessarily abide."

[7.3.1] Subputatio temporum ac solitudinis habitatio, cuius contemplatione conicis interioris hominis perfectionem nos consequi debuisse, hoc solummodo contulit nobis, ut disceremus quid esse nequeamus, non tamen fecit esse quod esse contendimus. nec enim aut desideratae puritatis fixam stabilitatem aut robur aliquod firmitatis nos hac scientia nouimus adsecutos, sed tantummodo confusionis ac pudoris augmenta.

[7.3.2] etenim cum omnium disciplinarum meditatio ad hoc cotidianis studiis exerceatur atque proficiat, ut a trepidis rudimentis ad peritiam certam stabilemque perueniens incipiat nosse quae primitus uel ambigue nouerat uel

FRUSTRATION

Cassian and Germanus Consult
Abba Serenus of Scetis

[Germanus said to Abba Serenus:] "You insist that we should have reached a perfect state of our inner person[27] by thinking about how long and how isolated our life as monks has been. But in doing this we've gotten just a single take-away: we have learned what we're incapable of being! It didn't actually make us become what we desperately wanted to be. We've come to realize that what we know hasn't helped us attain the steady and stable clarity we've been seeking, or any sort of hardiness—only more disorder and shame.

"Seriously: I make the effort every day to practice all our forms of discipline. I even succeed in these halting attempts to attain an expertise that's reliable and consistent, and I start to know what I'd only barely known or was totally

penitus ignorabat, et firmo ut ita dixerim gradu in illius disciplinae qualitate procedens perfecte in ea ac sine ulla iam difficultate uersetur, e contrario me in huius puritatis studio laborantem id solummodo profecisse repperio, ut sciam quid esse non possum. ex quo nihil mihi aliud sentio quam laborem tanta cordis contritione conferri, ut numquam scilicet desit materia lacrimarum nec tamen esse desinam quod esse non debeo.

[7.3.3] et idcirco quid profuit didicisse quod summum est, si cognitum nequeat adprehendi? nam cum directionem cordis ad destinata pertendere senserimus, insensibiliter mens inde reuoluta ad priores euagationes inpetu uehementiore prolabitur et ita cotidianis distentionibus occupata innumeris captiuitatibus incessanter abducitur, ut propemodum iam desperetur a nobis desiderata correctio et superflua haec obseruantia uideatur.

unaware of at first. I advance in the discipline and make what I'd call real progress, and things evolve perfectly, without a hitch. By contrast, when it comes to all the effort I've spent striving for a state of clarity, I've discovered that I've only advanced to the point of knowing what I *can't* be. Consequently I feel that I won't get anything out my heart's severe anguish, other than hard work. I'm never short on tearful feelings,[28] and yet I can't stop being the kind of person I shouldn't be.

"So what's the use of learning what's best if you can't actually obtain it? Even when we feel our heart heading straight toward its goals, the mind imperceptibly turns the other way, then in one intense paroxysm it backslides into its earlier meanderings. The daily claims on its attention mean that it's perpetually being taken captive, in a series of countless kidnappings, so at this point we've nearly lost hope of improving the situation, and our regimen seems completely ineffectual.

[7.3.4] siquidem per momenta singula lubricis discursibus animus euagatus cum ad timorem
dei uel contemplationem reducitur spiritalem,
priusquam firmetur in ea, rursum fugacius eua-
nescit, cumque eum uelut expergefacti depre-
henderimus ab intentione proposita deuiasse
atque ad illam theoriam unde discesserat redu-
centes uoluerimus eum tenacissima cordis intentione uelut quibusdam uinculis obligare, in ipso
conatu nostro ocius quam anguilla de recessibus
mentis elabitur.

[7.3.5] ob quam rem cotidianis huiusmodi ob-
seruationibus aestuantes nec tamen ex ipsis aliquod nostro cordi stabilitatis robur accessisse
cernentes ad hanc opinionem fracti desperatione
transducimur, ut non nostro iam, sed naturae
uitio has animae peruagationes humano generi
inesse credamus.

"If the distracted mind is occasionally led back from its slippery detours to a fear of God or to spiritual contemplation, it gains strength in those moments initially, but then it becomes even likelier to pull its vanishing acts. And when we come to and discover that our mind has deviated from what we'd planned to focus on, we want to lead it back to that contemplative practice it had deserted and bind it so extremely tightly with the attention of our heart that it's essentially handcuffed. But when we try to do that, it slips out of the mind's burrows, faster than an eel.

"The result is that we keep up these intense daily practices without seeing our heart become any more stable or strong. So now that our expectations have been dashed, we're drawn to this opinion: we believe that these profound distractions of the soul are present in the human species because of an inherent flaw, rather than any personal flaw on our part."

[7.4.1] SERENUS: Periculosae praesumptionis est necdum rebus recte discussis nec certa ratione collecta de natura cuiuslibet rei praepropere definire ac de consideratione fragilitatis suae capere coniecturam, non de statu et qualitate ipsius disciplinae uel de aliorum experientia proferre sententiam.

nec enim si quis natandi ignarus, sciens pondus corporis sui ferri aquarum liquore non posse, experimento suae uoluerit inperitiae definire neminem penitus posse liquidis elementis solida carne circumdatum sustineri, idcirco uera eius opinio iudicanda est, quam secundum experientiam suam uisus est protulisse, cum hoc non solum non esse inpossibile, sed etiam perfacile ab aliis fieri ratione certissima et oculorum fide non dubia conprobetur.

[7.4.2] νοῦς itquae, id est mens, ἀεικίνητος καὶ πολυκίνητος definitur, id est semper mobilis et

Serenus said: "It's dangerously presumptuous to jump to conclusions about the nature of something without having properly sorted out the issues or conducted a reliable analysis—let alone to speculate on the basis of one's own flimsy experience rather than drawing on the actual attributes and properties of the discipline in question, or on the experiential knowledge of other people, to reach a judgment.

"Say that someone didn't know how to swim and knew that the weight of his body couldn't be supported by water, then tried to conclude on the basis of his own lack of experience that nobody whose solid flesh was surrounded by liquid could possibly stay afloat! But his opinion shouldn't be validated. Not only is swimming not impossible; in fact it's really easy for some people. Relying on accurate analysis, and seeing it ourselves, proves this beyond a doubt.

"The *nous* or mind is defined as *aeikinētos kai polykinētos*, always and very much on the move.

multum mobilis. quod etiam in Sapientia quae
dicitur Salomonis aliis uerbis ita describitur: καὶ
γεῶδες σκῆνος βρίθει νοῦν πολυφρόντιδα, id est:
et terrenum habitaculum adgrauat mentem multa
cogitantem. haec igitur pro condicione naturae
numquam potest otiosa consistere, sed necesse
est eam, nisi prouisum habuerit ubi suos exerceat
motus et in quibus iugiter occupetur, propria
mobilitate discurrere et per omnia uolitare, donec
longo exercitio usuque adsuefacta diuturno,
quo uos in cassum dicitis laborare, experiatur et
discat quas memoriae suae materias debeat
praeparare, erga quas circumagat indefessos
uolatus et inmorandi robur adquirat, et ita praeualeat aduersas inimici suggestiones quibus distra-
hebatur extrudere atque in illo quem desiderat
statu et qualitate durare.

Solomon describes it in the Book of Wisdom in another way: *kai geōdes skēnos brithei noun polyphrontida*, 'And the earthly tabernacle weigheth down the mind that museth upon many things.' So because of its natural state it can't ever come to a standstill and do nothing. Unless it has some plan for where to direct its motion and how to keep itself busy, its inherent instability makes it run around and flit all over the place. Only after an extended period of training and habitual long-standing practice—which both of you are saying is pointless work!—will it gain the experience to learn what kind of things it should be outfitting its memory with.[29] Then it will fly in tireless circles around *those* memories and obtain the power of rootedness. And in doing so it will become strong enough to drive off the enemy's stimuli that used to pull it in different directions, and to firm up its character and its condition as it desires.

[7.4.3] non ergo hanc euagationem cordis nostri uel naturae humanae uel deo creatori eius debemus adscribere. uera est enim scripturae sententia, quia deus fecit hominem rectum: et ipsi quaesierunt cogitationes multas. a nobis ergo earum qualitas pendet, quia cogitatio, inquit, bona scientibus eam adpropinquat, uir autem prudens inueniet eam. quidquid enim ut inueniri possit nostrae prudentiae industriaeque subiectum est, si non fuerit inuentum, sine dubio nostrae desidiae uel inprudentiae, non naturae uitio reputandum est. cui sensui Psalmista quoque congruit dicens: beatus uir cui est auxilium eius abs te, domine: ascensus in corde suo disposuit. uidetis ergo in nostra dicione consistere, ut siue ascensus, id est pertingentes ad deum cogitationes, siue descensus, ad terrena scilicet et carnalia conruentes, in nostris cordibus disponamus.

[7.4.4] quae si non in nostra potestate consisterent, nec Pharisaeos dominus increpasset: quid cogitatis mala in cordibus uestris? nec per

"And so when our heart gets distracted we shouldn't chalk it up to human nature or to God, its creator. In fact scripture actually states that 'God made man upright. And they themselves have searched out many thoughts.' The essence of those thoughts depends on us, because as it says, 'a good thought will draw near to them who know it, and a prudent man will find it.' Since our ability to find something is predicated on our good sense and energy, *not* finding something should unquestionably be ascribed to laziness or ignorance, not to some defect of nature. The psalmist agrees with this idea too: 'Happy the man whose support is from you, O Lord; ascents he arranged in his heart.' So you see that we have firm control here: we determine in our hearts both the ascents—thoughts that reach out to God—and the descents—thoughts that sink into earthly and physical matters.

"And if our thoughts weren't within our power, the Lord wouldn't have rebuked the Pharisees: 'Wherefore think ye evil in your

prophetam praecepisset dicens: auferte malum
cogitationum uestrarum ab oculis meis, et: usque
quo morabuntur in te cogitationes noxiae? nec
in die iudicii earum qualitas quemadmodum
operum exigeretur a nobis, ita per Esaiam domino
conminante: ecce, inquit, ego uenio ut congre-
gem opera et cogitationes eorum cum omnibus
gentibus et linguis, sed ne condemnari quidem
earum testimonio uel defendi in illo terribili
atque metuendo examine secundum beati apostoli sententiam mereremur ita dicentis: et inter
se inuicem cogitationibus accusantibus aut etiam
defendentibus, in die qua iudicabit deus occulta
hominum secundum euangelium meum.

hearts?' He wouldn't have commanded through the prophet: 'Remove the evil of your thoughts before my eyes.' And 'How long are the thoughts of trouble within you?' We wouldn't be questioned about those thoughts along with our works on Judgement Day, as the Lord threatened through Isaiah: 'I am coming to gather their works and their thoughts with all the nations and their tongues.' And we certainly wouldn't deserve to be condemned or defended on the evidence of our thoughts in that terrifying and fearsome judgment, as the blessed apostle expressed it: 'and their thoughts between themselves accusing or also defending one another, in the day when God shall judge the secrets of men according to my gospel.'"

[9.2.1] Omnis monachi finis cordisque perfectio ad iugem atque indisruptam orationis perseuerantiam tendit, et quantum humanae fragilitati conceditur, ad inmobilem tranquillitatem mentis ac perpetuam nititur puritatem, ob quam omnem tam laborem corporis quam contritionem spiritus indefesse quaerimus et iugiter exercemus. et est inter alterutrum reciproca quaedam inseparabilisque coniunctio. nam sicut ad orationis perfectionem omnium tendit structura uirtutum, ita nisi huius culmine haec omnia fuerint conligata atque conpacta, nullo modo firma poterunt uel stabilia perdurare.

[9.2.2] quemadmodum enim sine illis adquiri uel consummari non potest haec de qua loquimur perpetua orationis iugisque tranquillitas, ita

WARMING UP FOR FIERY FOCUS

Cassian and Germanus Consult
Abba Isaac of Scetis

Isaac said: "The ultimate goal of every monk, and the process of honing the heart, point us in the direction of nonstop and uninterrupted perseverance in prayer, toward unshakeable mental calm and continuous clarity (human frailty permitting). Our inexhaustible pursuit of physical exertion and spiritual anguish, our nonstop training: we do it all for this. There's a certain mutual and unbreakable bond between the two. The structure of all our capabilities is engineered for praying perfectly, and at the same time, there's no way that these components can hold fast and steady unless they're framed and fastened to this king post of prayer.[30]

"The continuous and nonstop calm of prayer that we're talking about can't be obtained or accomplished without those capabilities, and

ne illae quidem uirtutes quae hanc praestruunt absque huius possunt adsiduitate conpleri. et ideo nec recte tractare de orationis effectu nec ad eius principalem finem, qui uniuersarum uirtutum molitione perficitur, subitanea disputatione poterimus intrare, nisi prius uniuersa, quae illius obtentu uel abscidenda sunt uel paranda, per ordinem dinumerata fuerint atque discussa, et secundum euangelicae parabolae disciplinam ea, quae ad spiritalis ac sublimissimae illius extructionem pertinent turris, subputata fuerint ac diligenter ante congesta.

[9.2.3] quae tamen nec proderunt praeparata nec recte superponi sibimet excelsa culmina perfectionis admittent, nisi egesto prius omni repurgio uitiorum et effossis succiduis mortuisque ruderibus passionum uiuae ut aiunt ac solidae terrae pectoris nostri, immo illi euangelicae petrae superiecta fuerint simplicitatis et humilitatis firmissima fundamenta, quibus haec turris

likewise, those capabilities that lay its foundation can't actually reach their full potential without persisting in prayer. So we can't accurately
deal with the effects of prayer, or jump into an
argument about its primary purpose (which is
accomplished by activating *all* our capabilities),
without first systematically enumerating and
dissecting everything that we should acquire or
throw out for prayer to prevail. Then we should
calculate and sort the supplies that, according
to the instructions in the Gospel parable, are
necessary for the construction of that sky-high
spiritual tower.

"However: once all those materials are pre-
pped, they won't really be at our disposal for
constructing and completing any soaring roof-
tops unless we first demolish our weaknesses.
But once we've dug up the dead and sunken de-
bris of the impulses that unsettle us, we can lay
an unshakeable foundation that is basic and
grounded,[31] on the living, solid earth (as they
say) of our breast—that rock in the Gospel.

spiritalium uirtutum molitionibus extruenda et inmobiliter ualeat stabiliri et ad summa caelorum fastigia confidentia propriae firmitatis adtolli.

[9.2.4] fundamentis etenim talibus innitentem, quamuis passionum imbres largissimi profundantur, quamuis ei persecutionum uiolenti torrentes instar arietis inlidantur, quamuis inruat et incumbat aduersariorum spirituum saeua tempestas, non solum ruina non diruet, sed nec ipsa aliquatenus uexabit inpulsio.

[9.3.1] Et idcirco ut eo feruore ac puritate qua debet emitti possit oratio, haec sunt omnimodis obseruanda. primum sollicitudo rerum carnalium generaliter abscidenda est, deinde nullius negotii causaeue non solum cura, sed ne memoria quidem penitus admittenda, detractationes, uaniloquia seu multiloquia, scurrilitates quoque

After the demolitions are done, *that's* the kind of foundation on which to build our tower of spiritual capacities. It will enable the tower to be completely stabilized and to be vaulted up to the summits of the heavens because its strength is so secure.

"Supported by a foundation like that, the tower won't collapse. It won't even be remotely rattled by external forces in the first place—no matter how much the torrential downpours of intrusive impulses rain down on it, no matter how much the violent bombardments of persecution hammer it like a battering ram, no matter how much the fierce storm of enemy spirits blows in and builds pressure.

"So in order to be able to utter a prayer with the intense heat and clarity that you should, here are the tasks you need to take care of. First of all, you need to mow down all your concerns for physical matters. Then you need to prune away your preoccupations about business matters and odd jobs, as well as gabbing, chitchatting, telling

similiter amputandae, irae prae omnibus siue tristitiae perturbatio funditus eruenda, concupiscentiae carnalis ac filargyriae noxius fomes radicitus euellendus.

[9.3.2] et ita his ac similibus uitiis extrusis penitus et abscisis, quae hominum quoque possunt patere conspectibus, talique ut diximus repurgii emundatione praemissa, quae simplicitatis et innocentiae puritate perficitur, iacienda sunt primum profundae humilitatis inconcussa fundamina, quae scilicet turrem intraturam caelos ualeant sustinere, deinde superponenda uirtutum spiritalis extructio et ab omni discursu atque euagatione lubrica animus inhibendus, ut ita paulatim ad contemplationem dei ac spiritales intuitus incipiat sublimari.

[9.3.3] quidquid enim ante orationis horam anima nostra conceperit, necesse est ut orantibus nobis per ingestionem recordationis occurrat.

dirty jokes, and other similar things that shouldn't get lodged in your memory. Above all, you need to dig deep to excavate the destabilizing forces of anger and sadness, and root out the toxic fire starter of impulsivity and greed.

"Once these and other weaknesses that people are prone to exhibit are cleared out and cut down—as I said, that's the preliminary work of clearing the construction site, which is accomplished through the clarifying effects of honesty and integrity—then it's time to lay the firm foundations of deep self-debasement. This is what can support a tower that makes its way to the heavens. Then on top of that you need to build a spiritual structure made of your moral strengths, and to keep your mind there, kept away from detours and slippery distractions, so that little by little it begins to be elevated to spiritual vistas and to the contemplation of God.

"Whatever our soul was thinking about before the hour of prayer, we'll inevitably run into an intrusive memory of it as we're praying.

quamobrem quales orantes uolumus inueniri, tales nos ante orationis tempus praeparare debemus. ex praecedenti enim statu mens in supplicatione formatur, eorundemque actuum procumbentibus nobis ad precem, uerborum quoque uel sensuum ante oculos imago praeludens aut irasci nos secundum praecedentem qualitatem aut tristari aut concupiscentias causasue praeteritas retractare aut risu fatuo, quod etiam pudet dicere, cuiusquam scurrilis dicti uel facti titillatione pulsari aut ad priores faciet uolitare discursus.

[9.3.4] et idcirco quidquid orantibus nobis nolumus ut inrepat, ante orationem de adytis nostri pectoris extrudere festinemus, ut ita illud apostolicum possimus inplere: sine intermissione orate, et: in omni loco leuantes puras manus sine ira et disceptatione. alias namque mandatum istud perficere non ualebimus, nisi mens nostra ab omni uitiorum purificata contagio uirtutibus

Consequently, we have to prepare ourselves in advance to end up praying the way we want to. The mind is shaped by the state it was in before it turned to prayer. And when we prostrate ourselves to pray, a visage appears before our eyes to reenact things we've already done or said or felt. Depending on what the prior experience was, it makes us mad or sad, or we rehash old tendencies and issues, or—I'm ashamed to say this—we burst out laughing at some dirty joke or gag, or we flit to our former distractions.

"For that reason, before we pray, we need to act fast to drive out from deep within ourselves whatever we don't want to sneak in while we're praying, so we might fulfill the apostolic command to pray without ceasing and pray everywhere, lifting up clean hands,[32] without wrath and doubting. We won't be able to carry it out otherwise, unless our mind is completely cleansed of contamination by its weaknesses and commits to its strengths as the only good

tantum uelut naturalibus bonis dedita iugi om-
nipotentis dei contemplatione pascatur.

[9.4.1] Etenim qualitas animae non inepte sub-
tilissimae plumae seu pennae leuissimae conparatur. quae si umoris cuiuspiam extrinsecus
accedentis corruptione uitiata non fuerit uel in-
fusa, mobilitate substantiae suae tenuissimi
spiritus adiumento uelut naturaliter ad sublimia
caelestiaque sustollitur. sin uero umoris cuiusquam aspargine uel infusione fuerit praegrauata, non modo in nullos aërios uolatus naturali
mobilitate raptabitur, sed etiam ad ima terrae
concepti umoris pondere deprimetur.

[9.4.2] ita mens quoque nostra si accedentibus
uitiis curisque mundanis adgrauata non fuerit
noxiaeue libidinis umore corrupta, uelut naturali
puritatis suae beneficio subleuata leuissimo spiritalis meditationis adflatu sublimabitur ad su-
perna, et humilia deserens atque terrena ad illa

things about it—so that it can feed on nonstop contemplation of the Almighty God.

"It's not a stretch to compare the state of the soul to the most delicate down or lightweight feather. If it isn't spoiled or saturated by some contaminating fluid coming into contact with it, the slightest breath sends its dynamic nature floating up to the highest heavens, like it's nothing. But if it's weighed down by some liquid that was sprinkled or poured on it, its inherent kinetic properties won't launch it into aerial flights in the same way. Instead the weight of the fluid it has absorbed will press it down to the depths of the earth.

"Our mind is like that, too. If it's not weighed down by flaws or by worldly concerns coming into contact with it, nor contaminated by the toxic fluid of desire, it will be lofted up to the heights by the lightest breeze of spiritual meditation, as if the natural boost of its tranquility were lifting it up; and as it leaves behind the

caelestia et inuisibilia transferetur. unde proprie
satis praeceptis dominicis admonemur: uidete ne
quando grauentur corda uestra in crapula et ebrietate et curis saecularibus.

[9.4.3] et idcirco si uolumus orationes nostras
non solum caelos, sed etiam ea quae super caelos
sunt penetrare, curemus mentem ab omnibus
terrenis uitiis expurgatam cunctisque mundatam
faecibus passionum ad subtilitatem perducere
naturalem, ut ita ad deum oratio eius nullo uitiorum pondere praegrauata conscendat.

[9.5.1] Notandum tamen quibus ex causis
grauari mentem dominus designauerit. non enim
adulteria, non fornicationes, non homicidia, non
blasphemias, non rapinas, quae mortalia esse et
damnabilia nullus ignorat, sed crapulam posuit
et ebrietatem et curas siue sollicitudines saeculares. quae in tantum nemo hominum mundi

lowly and earthly terrain, it is transported to the reaches of the celestial and invisible. We've been sufficiently warned about this very matter by the lordly injunctions: 'Take heed to yourselves, lest at any time your hearts be weighed down with surfeiting, and drunkenness, and cares of this life.'

"So if we want our prayers to reach not only the heavens but also what lies above the heavens, we should ensure that the mind is cleansed of every earthly flaw and dredged of all emotionally fraught sediment, to restore it to its natural lightness so that its prayer ascends to God without being weighed down by any weaknesses.

"We should take note of what the Lord identified as factors that weigh the mind down. He did not single out adultery, or other forms of extramarital sex, or murder, or contempt for the sacred, or robbery—which everyone knows are reprehensible, deathly serious offenses—but rather intoxication, overeating, and nonreligious

huius cauet aut damnabilia iudicat, ut etiam nonnulli, quod pudet dicere, semet ipsos monachos
nuncupantes isdem ipsis distentionibus uelut in-
noxiis et utilibus inplicentur.

[9.5.2] quae tria licet secundum litteram per-
petrata adgrauent animam atque a deo separent
ac deprimant ad terrena, est tamen eorum facilis
declinatio et maxime nobis, qui tam longa remo-
tione ab omni saeculi huius conuersatione disi-
ungimur et istis uisibilibus curis et ebrietatibus et
crapulis nulla penitus occasione miscemur.
uerum est alia quoque crapula non minus noxia
et ebrietas spiritalis difficilius euitanda, cura
quoque ac sollicitudo saecularis, quae nos etiam
post omnium facultatum nostrarum perfectam
renuntiationem et uini epularumque cunctarum
continentiam et quidem in solitudine constitutos

concerns and preoccupations. No human being on the planet is adequately wary or judgmental of these behaviors, to the point (I'm ashamed to say) that some people who call themselves monks are caught up in them as if they were harmless and even beneficial!

"Understood literally, these three acts weigh down the soul, separate it from God, and pin it to the earth. But it's easy to avoid them—especially for us monks, since we're so far removed that we're completely detached from all the world's dealings, and there's not really any opportunity to get mixed up with concerns about superficial things or intoxication or overeating. But there is another sort of excess that's no less toxic but harder to avoid. And that's *spiritual* drunkenness, a kind of 'nonreligious concern and preoccupation' that envelops us even after we've completely renounced all our property, and abstained from wine and feasts altogether, and spent a lot of time in isolation.

frequenter inuoluunt (de quibus propheta: ex-
pergiscimini, inquit, qui estis ebrii, et non a uino.

[9.5.3] alius quoque: obstupescite et admi-
ramini, fluctuate et uacillate: inebriamini, et non
a uino: mouemini, et non ebrietate. cuius ebri-
etatis uinum consequenter necesse est ut secundum prophetam furor draconum sit, ipsumque
uinum de qua radice procedat aduerte: ex uinea,
inquit, Sodomorum uitis eorum et sarmenta
eorum ex Gomorra.

[9.5.4] uis etiam fructum uitis istius atque sar-
menti germen agnoscere? uua eorum uua fellis,
botrus amaritudinis ipsis), quia omnino nisi
fuerimus cunctis uitiis expurgati et ab omnium
passionum crapula sobrii, absque ebrietate uini
epularumque omnium afluentia erit cor nostrum
ebrietate et crapula magis noxia praegrauatum.
nam quia saeculares curae etiam in nos, qui nullis actibus mundi istius admiscemur, cadere nonnumquam possint, manifesta ratione monstratur

The prophet spoke of this: 'Sober up, drunkards, and not from wine.'[33]

"Likewise another prophet said: 'Be astonished, and wonder, waver, and stagger: be drunk, and not with wine; stagger, and not with drunkenness.' Consequently, according to the prophet, the wine of *this* kind of drunkenness is none other than the wrath of the dragons. And notice the root from which this wine derives: 'their vine,' says the prophet, 'is from the vine of Sodoma, and their branch from Gomorra.'

"And do you want to know what the fruit of this vine and the bud of this branch are? Their cluster is a cluster of bile; it is a bunch of bitterness to them, because unless we're completely purged of all weaknesses and we've sobered up from our overindulgence in every pathology, our heart—despite foregoing extravagant banquets and intoxication from wine—will be weighed down by a much more toxic form of overeating and drunkenness. Nonreligious concerns can even paralyze those

secundum regulam seniorum, qui quidquid
necessitatem uictus cotidiani et ineuitabilem
usum carnis excedit, ad saecularem definierunt
curam et sollicitudinem pertinere:

[9.5.5] ut uerbi gratia si, cum possit operatio
unius solidi necessitatem nostri corporis expedire, ad duorum uel trium solidorum adquisitionem nosmet ipsos propensiore uelimus opere ac
labore distendere, et cum duarum uelamen sufficiat tunicarum ad usum scilicet noctis ac diei,
trium uel quattuor fieri domini procuremus,
cumque unius siue duarum habitatio sufficit cel-
lularum, ambitione saeculari atque amplitudine
delectati quattuor seu quinque cellas et has easdem exquisiti ornatus et capaciores quam usus
desiderat extruamus, passionem libidinis mundialis in quibus possumus praeferentes.

of us who don't get involved in the world's affairs. That clearly stands to reason, as the elders indicate through their way of life. They counted anything that exceeds the daily intake of food that one actually needs and what the body can't do without as a nonreligious concern and preoccupation.

"Here are some hypothetical examples. Say that a gold coin's worth of work is enough to meet our body's needs, but we'd rather prolong the time we spend on the job to earn two or three gold coins. Say that although two shirts are enough to clothe us—one for night and one for day—we buy three or four of them. And say that although a dwelling of one or two rooms is enough, our affinity for worldly striving and grandiosity leads us to build out four or five rooms that are beautifully decorated and much roomier than they need to be. In these scenarios, we are prioritizing the pathology of earthly desire whenever we can.

[9.6.1] Quod non sine instinctu daemonum fieri manifestissima nos experimenta docuerunt. nam quidam probatissimus seniorum cum transiret iuxta cellam cuiusdam fratris hac animi qua diximus aegritudine laborantis, utpote qui in extruendis reparandisque superfluis inquietus cotidianis distentionibus desudaret,

et eminus conspexisset eum graui malleo saxum durissimum conterentem uidissetque Aethiopem quendam adstantem illi et una cum eodem ictus mallei iunctis consertisque manibus inlidentem eumque ad operis illius instantiam ignitis facibus instigantem,

diutissime substitit uel inpressionem dirissimi daemonis uel fraudem tantae inlusionis admirans. [9.6.2] cum enim nimia lassitudine fatigatus frater requiescere iam finemque operi uoluisset inponere, instigatione spiritus illius

"Our experiences have taught us unambigu-
ously that this only ever happens at the demons'
instigation. For example: when one of the most
battle-tested of the elders went to visit the
dwelling of a certain brother, he saw that he was
sick with the kind of overworked mind that
we've been talking about: he was restlessly wearing himself out in the daily distractions of unnecessary busywork that he kept piling up for
himself.

"From a distance the elder spotted this monk
pounding on a really hard boulder with a big
mallet. He also saw an Ethiopian figure standing right next to him. They were hacking away
together as their hands interlocked on the mallet with each blow, and the figure was goading
the brother with lit torches to keep up the
work.[34]

"The elder stood there for a long time, riv-
eted by the horrible demon's assault and by the
sheer magnitude of the deception. When the
brother was worn out in utter exhaustion and

animatus iterum resumere malleum nec desinere
ab intentione coepti operis urguebatur, ita ut
isdem eius incitamentis infatigabiliter sustenta-
tus tanti laboris non sentiret iniuriam.

tandem igitur senex tam dira daemonis ludi-
ficatione permotus ad cellam fratris diuertit salu-
tansque eum, quod, inquit, est, frater, istud opus
quod agis?

at ille: laboramus, ait, contra istud durissimum saxum uixque illud potuimus aliquando
conterere.

[9.6.3] ad haec senex: bene dixisti "potuimus."
non enim solus eras, cum illud caederes, sed fuit
alius tecum quem non uidisti, qui tibi in hoc
opere non tam adiutor quam uiolentissimus in-
pulsor adstabat.

et idcirco morbum ambitus saecularis nostris
mentibus non inesse non utique eorum tantum
negotiorum abstinentia conprobabit, quae etiam

wanted to stop working and rest, he was reinvigorated by the spirit's goading to pick up the mallet again. And he was compelled to keep his attention on the work he'd started, so that his energy was sustained by the demon's directives, and he didn't notice how harsh the labor really was.

"Eventually the old man was so shaken by the demon's awful game that he made his way to the brother's dwelling, greeted him, and said: 'Brother! What's this work you're doing?'

"The brother said, 'We're toiling against this really hard boulder, and after all this time we've barely been able to chip anything off.'

"The old man replied, 'You're right to say *we*, because you weren't alone when you were hacking away. There was someone else with you whom you didn't see, someone who was standing right by you as you worked—not as a helper but as an oppressive taskmaster.'"

Isaac continued: "All of this is to say that 'giving up' dealings that we couldn't get involved

si uelimus expetere uel explere non possumus, neque illarum despectus rerum, quas si adfectauerimus tam apud spiritales uiros quam apud saeculi homines notabiles prima fronte reddemur, sed cum etiam illa, quae nostrae subpetunt potestati et honestate quadam uidentur obnubi, rigida mentis districtione respuimus.

[9.6.4] et re uera non minus haec, quae parua uidentur et minima quaeque ab his qui nostrae professionis sunt cernimus indifferenter admitti, pro qualitate sua adgrauant mentem, quam illa maiora quae secundum suum statum saecularium sensus inebriare consuerunt, non sinentes deposita faece terrena ad deum in quo semper defixa esse debet intentio monachum respirare, cui ab illo summo bono uel parua separatio mors praesens ac perniciosissimus interitus est credendus.

[9.6.5] cumque mens tali fuerit tranquillitate fundata uel ab omnium carnalium passionum

with or carry out even if we wanted to, or 're-jecting' things that, if we actually got involved with them, would shame us in the eyes of spiritual men and eminent laypersons alike, doesn't prove at all that the disease of worldly ambition isn't present in our minds! Instead we prove it by using stiff mental resistance to refuse to do things that *do* fall within our power and which pass as respectable.

"The fact is that things that seem minor and insignificant, things that monks like us let slide, don't inherently weigh down the mind any less than the major matters that tend to intoxicate the judgment of laypersons because they're so significant. As those earthly sediments build up, they make it hard for us to breathe easy as we turn to God, where a monk's attention should always be fastened. We should think of even the slightest separation from that greatest good as a sudden death and total annihilation.

"And when the mind is flooded with great calm and loosed from the shackles of all its

nexibus absoluta, et illi uni summoque bono tenacissima adhaeserit cordis intentio, apostolicum illud inplebit: sine intermissione orate, et:
in omni loco leuantes puras manus sine ira et
disceptatione. hac enim puritate, si dici potest,
sensu mentis absorto ac de terreno situ ad spiritalem atque angelicam similitudinem reformato
quidquid in se receperit, quidquid tractauerit,
quidquid egerit, purissima ac sincerissima erit
oratio.

[9.7.1] GERMANVS: Vtinam simili modo
atque eadem facilitate, qua semina spiritalium
cogitationum plerumque concipimus, etiam per-
petuitatem earum possidere possimus. cum
enim fuerint siue per memoriam scripturarum
seu per recordationem spiritalium quorumque
actuum uel certe per intuitum sacramentorum
caelestium nostro corde conceptae, insensibili
quadam fuga lapsae quantocius euanescunt.

[9.7.2] cumque alias quaslibet occasiones spiritalium sensuum mens nostra repperit, rursus

pathologies, and when the heart's attentiveness clings tenaciously to that one and greatest good, it will fulfill that apostolic command to pray without ceasing and pray everywhere, lifting up clean hands, without wrath and doubting. How can I put this? The mind becomes absorbed by this state of tranquility, and it morphs into a spiritual and angelic guise after having been stuck on the ground. No matter what it takes in or thinks about or does, its praying will be totally undistracted and undivided."

Germanus said: "If only we could retain the seeds of spiritual thoughts as easily as we first think of them—and to hold onto them forever! Instead, whether they enter our heart through a memory of the scriptures, a recollection of some spiritual accomplishment, or a glimpse of heavenly mysteries, it's only a matter of time before they make a run for it without us noticing, then disappear.

"Whenever our mind happens to have some encounter with spiritual perceptions, other

aliis inrepentibus ipsae quoque quae adprehen-
sae fuerant lubrica uolubilitate diffugiunt, ita ut
nullam constantiam sui retinens animus nec potestate propria sanctarum cogitationum pos-
sidens firmitatem etiam tunc, cum eas uidetur
utcumque retinere, fortuito illas et non de industria concepisse credatur. quomodo enim ortus
earum nostro arbitrio putabitur adscribendus,
quarum perseuerantia non consistit in nobis?

[9.7.3] sed ne forte sub huius quaestionis in-
dagine a coepto narrationis ordine longius eua-
gantes expositionem propositam super orationis
statu diutius retardemus, suo hanc tempori re-
seruantes de qualitate orationis instantissime
quaesumus informari, praesertim cum nullo tempore nos ab ea cessare beatus apostolus moneat
dicens: sine intermissione orate.

[9.7.4] et ideo primum de qualitate eius de-
sideramus institui, id est qualis debeat emitti

thoughts sneak in, causing the very things that the mind had seized on to make a slippery get-away, and scatter. The result is that the mind has no steadiness, no ability to keep its grip on spiritual thoughts. So even when it seems to be maintaining its hold on them, those moments of comprehension must be accidental rather than purposeful. How can the origin of these thoughts even be chalked up to our own decision making, given that their persistence has nothing to do with us?

"But we shouldn't wander way off the course of the subject we started by pursuing this line of questioning and further delay the discussion we'd intended to have about the logistics of prayer. Let's save that investigation for another time. We beg to be instructed this minute about what prayer involves, especially because the blessed apostle warned us never to take a break from it. As he said, 'Pray without ceasing.'

"First, we want to be educated about its basic features. Or in other words: what sort of prayer

semper oratio, deinde qualiter hanc eandem quaecumque est possidere uel exercere sine intermissione possimus. non enim parua cordis intentione eam perfici posse et experientia cotidiana et prosecutio tuae sanctitatis ostendit, qua finem monachi ac totius perfectionis culmen in orationis consummatione consistere definisti.

[9.8.1] ISAAC: Vniuersas orationum species absque ingenti cordis atque animae puritate et inluminatione sancti spiritus arbitror conprehendi non posse. tot enim sunt quot in una anima, immo in cunctis animabus status queunt qualitatesque generari.

[9.8.2] et ideo licet sciamus nos pro hebitudine cordis nostri uniuersas orationum species non posse perspicere, tamen, in quantum mediocritas experientiae nostrae adsequi praeualuerit, digerere eas utcumque temptabimus. secundum mensuram namque puritatis, in quam mens

should we always be sending out? Next: how can we possess and practice this prayer, whatever it is, without ceasing? Being able to achieve it requires more than a little attentiveness of the heart! We've learned as much from everyday experience and from your own holy affirmation. You've explained that the ultimate goal of the monk, and the summit of total perfection, depends on successful prayer."

Isaac said: "I think it's impossible to comprehend all the kinds of prayer there are without capaciousness of heart, stability of soul, and enlightenment from the Holy Spirit. There are as many kinds as there are circumstances and dispositions in a single soul—or really, in *all* souls.

"But even though we know that we can't ascertain all the types of prayer there are, because our heart isn't sharp enough, we will try to classify them somehow, as much as our limited experience allows. Even those types change from moment to moment, depending on the degree

unaquaeque proficit et qualitatem status in quo
uel ex accedentibus inclinatur uel per suam re-
nouatur industriam, ipsae quoque momentis
singulis reformantur: et idcirco uniformes orationes emitti semper a nemine posse certissi-
mum est.

[9.8.3] aliter enim quisque supplicat cum al-
acer est, aliter cum tristitiae seu desperationis
pondere praegrauatur, aliter cum spiritalibus successibus uiget, aliter cum inpugnationum mole
deprimitur, aliter cum ueniam peccatorum, aliter
cum adquisitionem gratiae seu cuiuslibet uirtutis
exposcit uel certe extinctionem cuiuscumque
uitii deprecatur, aliter cum consideratione gehennae ac futuri iudicii timore conpungitur, aliter
cum spe futurorum bonorum desiderioque flam-
matur, aliter cum in necessitatibus ac periculis,

of clarity that a mind attains, and on its current state (whether it's going downhill because of some incident, or whether it's making the effort to reenergize itself). This is why nobody can be absolutely sure that the prayers they're uttering are always the same.

"So people pray in one way when they're in a good mood, and in another way when they're weighed down with sadness or hopelessness, or thriving in their spiritual accomplishments, or pinned down under a pile of setbacks. They pray in one way when they're begging for their sins to be pardoned, and in another way when they want to obtain a favor or some other advantage, or when they're pleading to have a certain weakness eradicated for good. They pray in one way when they're stung by fear as they contemplate hell and future judgment, and in another way when they blaze with hope and longing for good things to come. They pray in one way when they're moved by need and

aliter cum in securitate ac tranquillitate uersatur, aliter cum sacramentorum caelestium reuelationibus inlustratur, aliter cum sterilitate uirtutum ac sensuum ariditate constringitur.

[9.9.1] Et idcirco his super orationum qualitate digestis, licet non quantum exposcit materiae magnitudo, sed quantum uel temporis admittit angustia uel certe capere tenuitas ingenii nostri et cordis praeualet hebitudo,

maior nobis nunc inminet difficultas, ut ipsas singillatim orationum species exponamus, quas apostolus quadripertita ratione distinxit ita dicens: deprecor itaque primo omnium fieri obsecrationes, orationes, postulationes, gratiarum actiones. quae non inaniter ab apostolo ita fuisse diuisa minime dubitandum est.

[9.9.2] et primitus indagandum quid obsecratione, quid oratione, quid postulatione, quid gratiarum actione signetur. deinde perquirendum

danger, and in another way when conversely they feel a sense of security and calm. They pray in one way when they're enlightened by visions of heavenly mysteries, and another way when they're short on strength and out of ideas.

"Okay, so we've noted some differences between prayers, but not as much as the sheer bulk of the subject matter demands. It's only as much as our short time allows and what our dull smarts and heart can really understand.

"Now it's time to deal with an even greater challenge: we need to lay out, one by one, the types of prayer that the apostle Paul divided into a four-part schema. As he put it, 'I exhort therefore, that, first of all, supplications, prayers, intercessions, and giving of thanks, be made.' Without a doubt, the apostle made these distinctions for a good reason.

"The first thing to investigate is what 'supplication,' 'prayer,' 'intercession,' and 'thanksgiving' mean. Then we should pursue the question

utrum hae quattuor species ab orante sint pariter
adsumendae, id est ut omnes simul in unaquaque
supplicatione iungantur, an uicissim singillat-
imque sint offerendae, ut puta nunc quidem
obsecrationes, nunc uero orationes, nunc autem
postulationes seu gratiarum actiones oporteat
promi, an certe alius quidem obsecrationes, alius
uero orationes, alius uero postulationes, alius
gratiarum actiones deo debeat exhibere secundum mensuram scilicet aetatis suae, in quam
unaquaeque mens per intentionis proficit
industriam.

[9.10] Et ideo primum proprietates ipsae sunt
nominum uerborumque tractandae ac discutien-
dum quid inter orationem et obsecrationem ac
postulationem intersit, deinde similiter perscru-
tandum utrum singillatim sint an pariter exhi-
bendae, tertio indagandum utrum etiam ipse
ordo qui ita est apostoli auctoritate dispositus
aliquid amplius instruat auditorem, an simpliciter accipienda sit ista distinctio et indifferenter

of whether the praying person should take on these four types at the same time. In other words, should all of them be yoked together in one single and simultaneous plea? Or should each one be offered up individually and con-secutively (which would mean having to start with supplications and moving on to prayers, then intercessions, then giving thanks)? Or should one person actually give God supplica-tions, another person prayers, another interces-sions, and another thanksgivings—depending on what stage a mind is in, when it's trying to pay attention?

"So the first thing to tackle are the particulari-ties of those nouns and verbs. We need to tease apart the differences between prayer and sup-plication and intercession. Then, continuing in this vein, we have to examine whether they should be practiced serially or simultaneously. Third, we have to investigate whether the exact order that the apostle authoritatively put them in has something more to teach the audience, or

putanda sit ab illo taliter fuisse digesta. quod mihi
satis uidetur absurdum. non enim credendum
est aliquid transitorie ac sine ratione spiritum
sanctum per apostolum protulisse. et idcirco
eodem quo coepimus ordine, prout dominus
donauerit, singula retractemus.

[9.11] Deprecor itaque primo omnium fieri
obsecrationes. obsecratio inploratio est seu pe-
titio pro peccatis, qua uel pro praesentibus uel
pro praeteritis admissis suis unusquisque con-
punctus ueniam deprecatur.

[9.12.1] Orationes sunt quibus aliquid offeri-
mus seu uouemus deo, quod Graece dicitur
εὐχή, id est uotum. nam ubi dicitur in Graeco
τὰς εὐχάς μου τῷ κυρίῳ ἀποδώσω, in Latino le-
gitur: uota mea domino reddam, quod secundum proprietatem uerbi ita exprimi potest: orationes meas domino reddam. et illud quod

whether we should take that list at face value and not think too much about whether he made those distinctions for some additional reason. I think this latter move is pretty clueless. We shouldn't buy into the idea that the Holy Spirit revealed something through the apostle so casually or uncalculatedly. Anyway, we'll go over each type one by one, in the order we started with, just as the Lord presented them.

"The apostle began: 'I exhort therefore, that, first of all, supplications be made.' A supplication is a call for help, or an appeal about sins. A person pleads for pardon with a supplication when they are stung with remorse about their past or present deeds.

"Prayers are what we present or vow to God. In Greek it's called *euchē*, or 'vow.' The Greek *tas euchas mou tō kyriō apodōsō* is read in Latin as 'I will pay my vows to the Lord,' which given the specific meaning of the word here could be expressed as 'I will pay my prayers to the Lord.' And the Latin verse we read in

legimus in Ecclesiaste: si uoueris uotum deo, ne moram feceris reddere illud, in Graeco similiter scribitur: ἐὰν εὔξῃ εὐχὴν τῷ κυρίῳ, id est: si oraueris orationem domino, ne moram feceris reddere illam.

[9.12.2] quod ita ab unoquoque nostrum inplebitur. oramus, cum renuntiantes huic mundo spondemus nos mortificatos cunctis actibus et conuersationi mundanae tota cordis intentione domino seruituros. oramus, cum pollicemur saeculari honore contempto ac terrenis opibus spretis in omni contritione cordis ac paupertate spiritus nos domino cohaesuros. oramus, cum promittimus nos purissimam corporis castitatem seu inmobilem patientiam exhibituros esse perpetuo, uel cum de corde nostro radices irae siue tristitiae mortem operantis uouemus funditus eruendas. quae cum desidia resoluti atque ad antiqua uitia recurrentes minime fecerimus,

Ecclesiastes—'Whenever you make a vow to God, do not delay to fulfill it'—is written in Greek in a similar way: *ean euxē euchēn tō kyriō*, or 'Whenever you pray a prayer to God, do not delay to fulfill it.'

"A monk would fulfill this command like so. We pray when, in renouncing this world, we pledge that we are dead to any engagement with it and to everything that happens in it, and that we will serve the Lord with the full attention of our heart. We pray when, after having rejected worldly prestige and spurned earthly wealth in a state of complete anguish of heart and poverty of spirit, we promise that we will be closely connected to the Lord. We pray when we make assurances that we will practice absolute bodily chastity and steadfast endurance forever, and when we vow to dig out the roots of anger and deadly sadness from the bottom of our heart. And when we barely do any of these things because we've gotten lazy and reverted to our old weaknesses, we will be held to account for our

erimus orationum nostrarum ac uotorum rei dice-
turque de nobis: melius est non uouere, quam
uouere et non reddere. quod secundum Graecum
dici potest: melius est non orare te, quam orare
et non reddere.

[9.13] Tertio loco ponuntur postulationes,
quas pro aliis quoque, dum sumus in feruore
spiritus constituti, solemus emittere, uel pro caris
scilicet nostris uel pro totius mundi pace poscen-
tes, et ut ipsius apostoli uerbis eloquar cum pro
omnibus hominibus, pro regibus et omnibus qui
in sublimitate sunt supplicamus.

[9.14] Quarto deinde loco gratiarum actiones
ponuntur, quas mens, uel cum praeterita dei recolit beneficia uel cum praesentia contemplatur,
seu cum in futurum quae et quanta praeparau-
erit deus his qui diligunt eum prospicit, per
ineffabiles excessus domino refert. qua etiam
intentione nonnumquam preces uberiores emitti

prayers and vows, and it will said about us: 'It is better that you do not vow than that you vow and do not pay up.' Or following the Greek, it could be put this way: 'It is better that you do not pray than that you pray and do not pay up.'

"Intercessions come third. We tend to utter these on behalf of other people, when our spirit is in a state of intense heat. We intercede in making requests for our loved ones or for peace across the entire world, and when we are making entreaties (and I will quote the apostle's own words here) 'for all men, for kings, and for all that are in authority.'

"Then, in fourth place, are thanksgivings. The mind gives thanks to the Lord out of a sense of indescribable ecstasy[35] — when it recalls God's previous acts of support, or contemplates present ones, or looks forward to the many things that God will provide in the future for those who love him. And sometimes in this form of attentiveness even richer prayers are

solent, dum illa quae reposita sunt in futuro sanctorum praemia purissimis oculis intuendo ineffabiles deo gratias cum inmenso gaudio spiritus noster instigatur effundere.

[9.15.1] Ex quibus quattuor speciebus licet nonnumquam soleant occasiones supplicationum pinguium generari (nam et de obsecrationis specie quae de conpunctione nascitur peccatorum, et de orationis statu quae de fiducia oblationum et consummatione uotorum pro conscientiae profluit puritate, et de postulatione quae de caritatis ardore procedit, et de gratiarum actione quae beneficiorum dei et magnitudinis ac pietatis eius consideratione generatur, feruentissimas saepissime nouimus preces ignitasque prodire, ita ut constet omnes has quas praediximus species omnibus hominibus utiles ac necessarias inueniri, ut in uno eodemque uiro nunc quidem obsecrationum, nunc autem orationum, nunc postulationum puras ac feruentissimas supplicationes uariatus emittat affectus),

uttered. In the act of gazing, clear-eyed, on the rewards that are in store for the holy, our spirit is stirred with boundless joy to pour out its indescribable thanks to God.

"These four types of prayer can sometimes produce juicy[36] moments of solemnity. The type of supplication born from sinners' stinging sense of remorse, and the kind of prayer that flows from a place of trust in what's being offered up and from vows performed with clear self-awareness, and the intercession that comes from the heat of love, and the thanks that are produced by reflecting on God's acts of support and on his greatness and devotion: we know that they generate whitehot, fiery prayers all the time. So we can obviously conclude that all the types of prayers we talked about earlier are useful and essential to everybody. One and the same man, depending on his mood, may make clear and white-hot entreaties that sometimes take the form of supplications, sometimes prayers, sometimes intercessions.

tamen prima ad incipientes uidetur peculiarius pertinere, qui adhuc uitiorum suorum aculeis ac memoria remordentur, secunda ad illos qui in profectu iam spiritali adpetituque uirtutum quadam mentis sublimitate consistunt, tertia ad eos qui perfectionem uotorum suorum operibus adinplentes intercedere pro aliis quoque consideratione fragilitatis eorum et caritatis studio prouocantur, quarta ad illos qui iam poenali conscientiae spina de cordibus uulsa securi iam munificentias domini ac miserationes, quas uel in praeterito tribuit uel in praesenti largitur uel praeparat in futuro, mente purissima retractantes ad illam ignitam et quae ore hominum nec conprehendi nec exprimi potest orationem feruentissimo corde raptantur.

[9.15.2] nonnumquam tamen mens, quae in illum uerum puritatis proficit adfectum atque in

"That said, the first type of prayer seems especially well suited to beginners who are still tormented by their memory and by the stings of their weaknesses. The second type suits people whose minds are somewhat elevated because they've already started a spiritual undertaking and want to get stronger. The third is for people who have done the work and made good on their vows, whose sense of love and consideration for the vulnerability of other people rouse them to intercede for others, too. And the fourth is for people who are untroubled by the punishing thorn of self-consciousness: it has been pulled out of their hearts. They keep thinking, in their perfectly clear mind, about the Lord's acts of generosity and compassion that he granted in the past, bestows in the present, and plans for the future. And their white-hot heart carries them off to that state of fiery prayer that no human mouth can encapsulate or describe.

"However: sometimes a mind, a mind that's making progress in that genuine state of clarity

eo iam coeperit radicari, solet haec omnia simul
pariterque concipiens atque in modum cuiusdam inconprehensibilis ac rapacissimae flammae
cuncta peruolitans ineffabiles ad deum preces
purissimi uigoris effundere, quas ipse spiritus
interpellans gemitibus inenarrabilibus ignoran-
tibus nobis emittit ad deum, tanta scilicet in illius horae momento concipiens et ineffabiliter
in supplicatione profundens, quanta non dicam
ore percurrere, sed ne ipsa quidem mente ualeat
alio tempore recordari.

[9.15.3] et inde est, quod in qualibet mensura
quis positus nonnumquam puras intentasque
preces inuenitur emittere, quia et de illo primo
et humili ordine, qui est super recordatione futuri
iudicii, is qui adhuc sub terroris est poena ac metu
examinis constitutus ita ad horam conpungitur,
ut non minore spiritus alacritate de obsecrationis pinguedine repleatur, quam ille qui per puritatem cordis sui munificentias dei perlustrans

and has already begun to take root there, starts thinking about all these things all at once, and it flits around all over the place like some elusive, furious flame. It will pour out wordless prayers of sheer energy to God, prayers that the Spirit itself intercepts and sends straight to God with groanings that we cannot perceive or utter. In that moment, the mind is thinking about so many things and pouring them out in the act of prayer that, I think, the mouth couldn't express all of it. Not even the mind itself could remember it all after the fact.

"That's why someone can end up uttering prayers that are clear and attentive regardless of what stage they're in. Because even at that first and most amateur level, which involves dwelling on future judgment, a person who lives under the torment of dread is so struck with the fear of that final audit that they're filled with remorse on the spot. As a result they're filled with the juiciness of a supplication—no less alert in spirit than a person who surveys and

atque percurrens ineffabili gaudio laetitiaque resoluitur. incipit enim secundum sententiam domini plus diligere, quia sibimet ampliora cognoscit indulta.

[9.16] Tamen expetendae sunt nobis per profectum uitae consummationemque uirtutum illae potius supplicationum species, quae uel de contemplatione futurorum bonorum uel de caritatis ardore funduntur seu certe, ut humilius et secundum incipientium mensuram loquar, pro adquisitione quarumcumque uirtutum seu uitii cuiuslibet extinctione generantur. aliter enim ad illa sublimiora quae praediximus supplicationum genera peruenire nullatenus poterimus, nisi per ordinem postulationum istarum sensim mens nostra fuerit gradatimque prouecta.

reviews all of God's acts of generosity with a clear heart then melts into indescribable happiness and celebration. They begin to love much, as the Lord put it, because they recognize that they have been forgiven for many things.

"Even so, as we advance in life and become more proficient we should prefer to strive for the types of prayers that are poured out from contemplating good things to come, or from the heat of love, or in any case—if I'm speaking in less vaunted terms, out of consideration for beginners' limitations—prayers that are born of the effort to attain some particular ability or eradicate some deficiency. Otherwise there's no way we'd be able to reach those exalted kinds of prayer that we mentioned earlier. It will happen only if our mind progresses through those prayers in order, little by little and step by step."

[9.26.1] Quis uero possit diuersitates et causas ipsas atque origines conpunctionum quantalibet experientia praeditus sufficienter exponere, quibus inflammata mens atque succensa ad orationes puras ac feruentissimas incitatur? quarum pauca, quantum potuerimus ad praesens per inluminationem domini reminisci, exempli gratia proponemus.

nonnumquam etenim psalmi cuiuscumque uersiculus occasionem orationis ignitae decantantibus nobis praebuit. interdum canora fraternae uocis modulatio ad intentam supplicationem stupentium animos excitauit. [9.26.2] nouimus quoque distinctionem grauitatemque psallentis etiam adstantibus plurimum contulisse feruoris. nec non exhortatio uiri perfecti et conlatio spiritalis frequenter ad uberrimas preces iacentium erexit affectum. scimus etiam fratris seu cari cuiuslibet interitu non minus nos ad plenam conpunctionem fuisse raptatos. recordatio

LATER IN THE CONVERSATION WITH ISAAC

Isaac continued: "Who is so experienced that they are capable of adequately enumerating the whole range of catalysts and sources of the intense feelings[37] that move a kindled and crackling mind to clear and white-hot prayers? I'll give a few examples of them, as many as I'm able to remember at the moment with some illumination from the Lord.

"Sometimes a short verse from a psalm we're chanting presents an opportunity for fiery prayer. Occasionally a brother's melodious singing will animate inactive minds to pray attentively. We also know that a distinguished and serious chanter can really heat up a congregation. And when people feel downcast, encouragement from accomplished men, and spiritual consultation with them, often elevates their mood to produce extremely productive prayers. We also know that we're likely to be seized by full-blown sorrow when a brother or other

quoque teporis ac neglegentiae nostrae nonnumquam nobis salutarem spiritus inuexit ardorem. atque in hunc modum nulli dubium est
occasiones innumeras non deesse, quibus per dei
gratiam tepor ac somnolentia nostrarum men-
tium ualeat excitari.

[9.27] Quemadmodum uero uel quibus modis
istae ipsae conpunctiones de intimis animae con-
clauibus proferantur, non minoris difficultatis est
indagare. frequenter enim per ineffabile gaudium
et alacritatem spiritus saluberrimae conpunctionis fructus emergit, ita ut etiam in clamores
quosdam intolerabilis gaudii inmensitate pro-
rumpat et cellam uicini iucunditas cordis et ex-
ultationis penetret magnitudo. nonnumquam
uero tanto silentio mens intra secretum profundae taciturnitatis absconditur, ut omnem penitus sonum uocis stupor subitae inluminationis
includat omnesque sensus adtonitus spiritus uel
contineat intrinsecus uel amittat ac desideria sua
gemitibus inenarrabilibus effundat ad deum. interdum uero tanta conpunctionis abundantia ac

loved one dies. And sometimes even the recollection of our lukewarmness and carelessness
induces a healthy heat in our spirit. So there's
obviously no shortage of situations in which the
lukewarmness and sleepiness of our minds can
be stirred with God's help.

"But it's no small challenge to investigate
how these situations actually draw such intense
feelings out of the deep chambers of the soul.
This most nutritious fruit of feeling often appears in a moment of inexpressible joy and
spiritual transport, so that it erupts into audible
shouts because the joy is so irresistibly great, and
the heart's enjoyment and noisy excitement can
be heard by the monk next door. Or sometimes
the mind is so still, tucked away within a hiding
place of deep silence, that a sudden flash of insight will completely mute the voice; and the
stunned spirit either withdraws all its sense perceptions into itself or loses them entirely, and it
pours out its desires to God with inexpressible
lamentations. And occasionally it's so filled to

dolore suppletur, ut alias eam digerere nisi lacrimarum euaporatione non possit.

[9.28.1] GEMANVS: Hunc equidem conpunctionis affectum ex parte aliqua mea quoque
exiguitas non ignorat. frequenter enim recordatione delictorum meorum obortis lacrimis ita
sum hoc ineffabili ut praefatus es gaudio uisi-
tante domino uegetatus, ut desperare me illorum ueniam non debere laetitiae ipsius magnitudo dictaret. quo statu reor nihil esse sublimius,
si reparatio eius nostro subiaceret arbitrio.

[9.28.2] nam nonnumquam cupiens ad similem
me lacrimarum conpunctionem totis uiribus ex-
citare omnesque errores meos atque peccata
ante oculos statuens ubertatem illam fletuum
reuocare non possum, et ita oculi mei in
modum cuiusdam durissimae silicis praedurant-
tur, ut nulla prorsus ex eis umoris gutta des-
tillet. et ideo quantum mihi in illa lacrimarum

the brim with feeling and pain that the only way to handle it is to cry until there are no tears left."[38]

Germanus said, "From my perspective, even lightweights like me know something of this intense feeling. Tears often spring up when I recall the wrongs I've done, so that just as you've said, I'm enlivened by this inexpressible joy in the Lord's presence. And the sheer immensity of this celebratory mood suggests that I shouldn't lose hope that my wrongs will be pardoned. I don't think anything is more sublime than such an experience—if only it were within our control to have it again!

"And that's the thing. Sometimes when I want to rouse myself with all my might to that same intense feeling, I set all my mistakes and sins before my eyes. But I just can't summon that wave of weeping again, and my eyes remain unmoved like some insensate rock: not a single drop of moisture trickles out of them! As much as I rejoiced in that prior flood of tears,

profusione congaudeo, tantum doleo quod illam, cum uoluero, recuperare non possum.

[9.29.1] ISAAC: Non omnis lacrimarum profusio uno adfectu uel una uirtute depromitur. aliter enim ille emanat fletus, qui peccatorum spina cor nostrum conpungente profertur, de quo dicitur: laboraui in gemitu meo, lauabo per singulas noctes lectum meum: lacrimis stratum meum rigabo, et iterum: deduc quasi torrentem lacrimas per diem et per noctem: et non des requiem tibi, neque taceat pupilla oculi tui:

[9.29.2] aliter qui de contemplatione aeternorum bonorum et desiderio futurae illius claritatis exoritur, pro qua etiam uberiores lacrimarum fontes de intolerantia gaudii et alacritatis inmensitate prorumpunt, dum sitit anima nostra ad deum fortem uiuum dicens: quando ueniam et apparebo ante conspectum dei? fuerunt mihi lacrimae meae panis die ac nocte, cum heiulatu cotidie et lamentatione proclamans: heu mihi, quod incolatus meus prolongatus est, et: multum incola fuit anima mea.

I'm just as distressed about not being able to re-
cover it whenever I want to."

Isaac replied, "Not every flood of tears is
induced by the same mood or force. Sometimes
we shed tears when prompted by the thorn of
sins pricking our heart. As it's said, 'I'm weary
with my groaning; all the night make I my bed
to swim; I water my couch with my tears.' And
again: 'Let tears run down like a river day and
night: give thyself no rest; let not the apple of
thine eye cease.'

"Sometimes it arises when we're thinking
about everlasting good things and we're longing
for that splendor to come. This lets loose deep
springs of tears from a place of unbearable joy
and overwhelming anticipation, while our thirsty
soul says to the powerful living God, 'When
shall I come and appear before God? My tears
have been my bread day and night.' And every
day it cries out with wailing and weeping, 'Woe
is me that my place of sojourn was put at a distance, and very much did my soul sojourn.'

[9.29.3] aliter profluunt lacrimae, quae absque ulla quidem letalium criminum conscientia,
sed tamen de metu gehennae et terribilis illius
iudicii recordatione procedunt, cuius terrore
propheta perculsus orat ad deum non intres, inquiens, in iudicio cum seruo tuo: quia non ius-
tificabitur in conspectu tuo omnis uiuens. est
etiam aliud lacrimarum genus, quod non pro
sua conscientia, sed pro aliena duritia pec-
catisque generatur: quo Samuhel Saulem, quo
illam quoque ciuitatem Hierusalem uel dominus in euangelio uel in praeteritis Hieremias
fleuisse describitur, ita dicens: quis dabit capiti
meo aquam, et oculis meis fontem lacrimarum?
et plorabo in die et in nocte interfectos filiae
populi mei.

[9.29.4] uel certe quales illae sunt lacrimae, de
quibus in psalmo centensimo primo canitur: quia
cinerem sicut panem manducaui, et poculum
meum cum fletu miscebam. quas certum est non
illo adfectu promi, quo in sexto psalmo ex persona

"Sometimes the tears flow even when we don't have any serious crimes on our conscience. But they start up out of fear of Gehenna all the same, when we remember that terrifying trial that struck the prophet with dread. He prayed to God, 'Enter not into judgment with thy servant: for in thy sight shall no man living be justified.' And there is another category of tears that doesn't come from self-awareness but rather from other people's sins and their lack of feeling. This is how Samuel wept over Saul, or likewise how the Lord in the Gospel wept over the city of Jerusalem, or as Jeremiah once said, 'Who will give my head water and my eyes a fountain of tears, and I shall bewail my people day and night, the slain of the daughter of my people?'

"These are unquestionably the kind of tears about which Psalm 101 sings, 'For I have eaten ashes like bread, and mingled my drink with weeping.'[39] They're certainly not prompted by that feeling that causes the penitent figure to

paenitentis emergunt, sed pro anxietatibus uitae huius atque angustiis et aerumnis, quibus iusti in hoc mundo positi deprimuntur. quod etiam psalmi ipsius non solum textus, sed etiam titulus euidenter ostendit, qui ex persona pauperis illius de quo in euangelio dicitur: beati pauperes spiritu, quoniam ipsorum est regnum caelorum, ita describitur: oratio pauperis, cum anxiatus fuerit, et coram deo effuderit precem suam.

[9.30.1] Ab his ergo lacrimis multum distant illae quae obdurato corde de siccis oculis exprimuntur. quas licet non penitus infructuosas esse credamus (bono enim proposito earum adtemptatur emissio, ab his praesertim qui necdum uel ad scientiam peruenire perfectam uel pristinorum seu praesentium uitiorum potuerunt ad purum labe mundari), ab his tamen qui in affectum iam transiere uirtutum nequaquam debet hoc modo extorqueri profusio lacrimarum nec exterioris

weep in Psalm 6—but rather by the anxiety and distress and worry about this life that weigh down ethical people in this world. Both the text of Psalm 101 and its title makes this obvious: *The Prayer of a Poor Person When He Is Worried and Pours Out His Prayer before God.* The Gospel describes that figure: 'Blessed are the poor in spirit, for theirs is the kingdom of heaven.'

"Tears of that kind are very different from the tears that a hard heart squeezes out from dry eyes. That said, we shouldn't think of this latter kind of tears as completely useless: people who try aggressively to shed them are well intentioned enough, given that they haven't yet been able to achieve complete knowledge or to be totally cleansed of the contaminant of their past or present weaknesses. But people who have already begun to feel the influence of positive forces within themselves definitely shouldn't wring out tears like this, and they

hominis magno opere adfectandi sunt fletus, qui etiamsi fuerint utcumque producti, numquam pertingere illam spontanearum lacrimarum poterunt ubertatem.

[9.30.2] magis enim supplicantis animum suis conatibus detrahentes humiliabunt atque ad humana demergent et ab illa caelesti sublimitate deponent, in qua adtonita mens orantis indeclinabiliter debet esse defixa, eamque conpellent precum suarum intentione laxata erga steriles et coacticias lacrimarum guttulas acgrotare.

[9.31] Et ut orationis uerae percipiatis adfectum, non meam uobis, sed beati Antoni sententiam proferam. quem ita nonnumquam in oratione nouimus perstitisse, ut eodem in excessu mentis frequenter orante cum solis ortus coepisset infundi, audierimus eum in feruore spiritus proclamantem: quid me inpedis, sol, qui ad hoc iam oreris, ut me ab huius ueri luminis abstrahas claritate?

shouldn't make a whole production of trying to cry. Even if they somehow manage it, they'd never attain that richness that comes with tears shed spontaneously.

"And what's more: in trying to pray like this they will sink even lower, as they drag down the mind, pull it from that heavenly peak (where the thunderstruck mind should be unbendingly fastened in prayer), plunge it into mortal matters, and force it to languish in empty, compulsory droplets of tears once its attention to its prayers goes slack.

"In order for you to make sense of what true prayer feels like, I'll quote the blessed Antony rather than myself. We know that sometimes he remained so steadfast in prayer that his mind was often transported, and when the sun's rays would just start to pour over the horizon, we'd hear him calling out as his spirit fumed: 'Sun! Why are you getting in my way?! You're rising just to drag me away from the brightness of the true light!'

cuius etiam haec quoque est super orationis fine caelestis et plus quam humana sententia: non est, inquit, perfecta oratio, in qua se monachus uel hoc ipsum quod orat intellegit. . . .

"Antony also said something about the ultimate goal of prayer, in words that were more heavenly than human: 'Perfect prayer is a state in which a monk is unaware of himself and the fact that he's praying at all.'"

[10.8.1] GERMANVS: Maior nobis ad praeteritae conlationis illius admirationem, ob quam huc recurrimus, magnitudo stuporis adcrescit. quantum enim incitamento doctrinae huius ad desiderium perfectae beatitudinis inflammamur, tantum maiore desperatione concidimus, ignorantes quemadmodum disciplinam tantae sublimitatis expetere uel obtinere possimus. quapropter quae in cella positi diutina meditatione uoluere coeperamus, quia necesse est loquaci forsitan prosecutione proferri, quaesumus ut explicari ea a nobis patienter admittas, quamquam sciamus beatitudinem tuam nullis solere offendi ineptiis infirmorum, quae uel ob hoc sunt in medium proferendae, ut quae in eis absurda sunt corrigantur.

A MANTRA

Cassian and Germanus Consult Abba Isaac Again

Germanus said, "We are parts amazed and dazed by our prior conversation with you, which is why we came back here. As excited as we are by this teaching, as much as it makes us long for a state of complete bliss, we've lowered our expectations that much more, because we don't know how we can possibly strive for—let alone achieve—such exalted conduct. Maybe this calls for a lengthy follow-up? We had started going over and over all of this in a long meditation in our cell, and we beg you to put up with us as we unpack it all (which isn't to say that your blessed self usually gets irritated with needy and presumptuous people!). This way everything will be laid out on the table, so whatever screwy ideas we've got can be set straight.

[10.8.2] quantum itaque opinio nostra sese habet, cuiuslibet artis seu disciplinae perfectio necesse est ut a quibusdam mollibus incipiens rudimentis facilioribus primum ac tenerrimis initiis inbuatur, ut quodam rationabili lacte nutrita paulatim educataque succrescat atque ita ab imis ad summa sensim gradatimque conscendat: quibus cum fuerit planiora principia et quodammodo ianuas adreptae professionis ingressa, ad penetralia quoque perfectionis et excelsa fastigia consequenter et absque labore perueniat.

[10.8.3] nam quemadmodum pronuntiare puerorum quispiam simplices poterit copulas syllabarum, nisi prius elementorum characteres diligenter agnouerit? uel quomodo citatam legendi peritiam consequetur, qui breues et perangustas descriptiones nominum necdum est idoneus coniugare? qua autem ratione is qui peritia grammaticae disciplinae minus instructus est uel

"So okay, here's the impression we have. When it comes to perfecting a given craft or discipline, it's essential in the early stages to be trained with beginner-level exercises that are easier, forgiving, and very low impact. Gradually, a person will grow when raised in this way, nursed on a kind of milk of reason: little by little, step by step, they will climb from the depths to the heights. And when they've made it through this accessible introductory training and passed through the 'doors' of the profession they've taken up, they will eventually summit the innermost and highest trails of perfection, without even breaking a sweat.

"After all, how could children learn to pronounce simple sequences of syllables without first really knowing the letters of the alphabet? How would they go on to be fast readers if they aren't yet capable of grouping short phrases together? How in the world would someone who isn't educated in grammar attain the fluency of rhetoric or the knowledge of philosophy?

rhetoricam facundiam uel philosophicam scientiam consequetur? quapropter huic quoque
sublimissimae disciplinae, per quam instruimur
deo iugiter inhaerere, non dubito quaedam in-
stitutionis inesse fundamina, quibus primum
firmissime conlocatis post haec superposita
extollantur perfectionis excelsa fastigia.

[10.8.4] cuius haec esse principia tenuiter sus-
picamur, ut primum nouerimus qua meditatione
teneatur uel cogitetur deus, deinde hanc eandem
quaecumque est materiam quemadmodum ualeamus inmobiliter custodire, quod etiam non
ambigimus culmen totius perfectionis exsistere.
et idcirco quandam memoriae huius materiam,
qua deus mente concipiatur uel perpetuo teneatur, nobis cupimus demonstrari, ut eam prae
oculis retentantes, cum elapsos nos ab eadem
senserimus, habeamus in promptu quo resipis-
centes ilico reuertamur ac resumere illam sine
ulla circuitus mora et inquisitionis difficultate
possimus.

I'm sure that the same is true of this incomparably exalted discipline, through which we're taught to cling tightly to God nonstop. Certain educational foundations need to be set solidly in place first. Then the framework of perfection can be built on top of them and sent soaring.

"Our tentative theory is that these are the beginning steps: first, we need to figure out what exactly we should be reciting to grasp and think about God. Then, we should keep a very close watch on this material,[40] whatever it might be, because we have no doubts that the peak of complete perfection will come into view. So we want you to show us what this methodological stuff of the memory actually is—the material that the mind uses to perceive and hold on to God constantly. That way we can keep it right in front of our eyes, and when we notice that we've fallen away from it, it will be easily accessible when we snap back to attention and get

[10.8.5] euenit namque, ut cum de theoriis spiritalibus euagati ad nosmet ipsos uelut de letali sopore conuertimur et tamquam experge-facti materiam quaerimus, qua illam quae ob-ruta est spiritalem memoriam resuscitare possimus, rctardati ipsius inquisitionis mora, priusquam repperiamus eam, a nostro conatu iterum deuoluamur, et antequam spiritalis quidam pariatur intuitus, concepta cordis eua-nescat intentio. quam confusionem idcirco nobis accidere satis certum est, quia speciale aliquid prae oculis propositum uelut formulam quan-dam stabiliter non tenemus, ad quam possit uagus animus post multos anfractus ac discur-sus uarios reuocari et post longa naufragia uelut portum quietis intrare.

[10.8.6] itaque fit ut hac ignoratione ac dif-ficultate mens iugiter praepedita errabunda

right back to work. We'll be able to pick it up again without going around in circles or looking all over the place.

"Because, I mean, the way things go now is that when we've gotten distracted from spiritual contemplation, then come to, it's like we've awakened from a deathly sleep. Then we have to go looking for a guide we can use to recuperate the spiritual memory that sank out of sight. There is a prolonged search, and before we find it we falter again; and before we obtain some spiritual perspective, the attention held in our heart slips away. It's pretty clear that this disorientation befalls us because we don't have some particular thing set in front of our eyes to hold tight to—like a rule of thumb or something the wandering mind can work its way back to after so many different digressions and detours, like entering a serene harbor after grueling storms at sea.

"So the result is that the mind is constantly tangled up in this ignorant and struggling state,

semper et uelut ebria per diuersa iactetur et ne
illud quidem quod casu potius quam industria
sibimet occurrerit spiritale diu ac firmiter teneat, dum aliud ex alio semper recipiens sicut
introitus eorum atque principia, ita etiam finem
discessumque non sentiat.

[10.9.1] ISAAC: Inquisitio uestra tam minuta
atque subtilis proximae puritatis praesignat indicium. nec enim de his saltim interrogare, non
dicam introspicere atque discernere quispiam
praeualebit, nisi quem diligens et efficax mentis
industria ac sollicitudo peruigil ad perscrutan-
dam istarum profunditatem prouexerit quaes-
tionum castigataeque uitae iugis intentio per
experientiam fecerit actualem adtemptare puritatis huius limina ianuasque pulsare.

[10.9.2] et idcirco quoniam uideo uos non
dicam pro foribus orationis illius uerae de qua
disserimus adstitisse, sed ipsis quodammodo experientiae manibus penetralia eius et interiora

always reeling around and stumbling into things like it's drunk. And as long as it keeps starting one thing after another and never seeing anything through to the end, it won't hold tight for very long—not even to some spiritual thing it happens to run into accidentally rather than intentionally!"

Isaac said: "You've put the problem in a fine-grained and precise way, and it's a sign that clarity is close by. But no one will prevail with this line of questioning (let alone pick things apart and get to the bottom of them) unless they carry it out with assiduous and powerful mental effort and with an unblinking commitment to investigating these deep matters. Nonstop attentiveness to self-correction is the practical experience that will enable you to march right up to the threshold of clarity and knock on the door.

"So I wouldn't say that I see you standing *outside* the doors of that form of prayer we've talked about. It's more like you're already feeling your way through its inner passageways with

palpare et quaedam membra iam iamque con-
tingere, nec me laboraturum credo, ut iam
intra aulam quodammodo ipsius oberrantes in
adyta quoque, in quantum dominus direxerit,
introducam, nec uos ad introspicienda haec quae
demonstranda sunt ullo difficultatis obstaculo
retardandos.

[10.9.3] proximus enim cognitioni est, qui
quid inquirere debeat prudenter agnoscit, nec a
scientia longe est, qui coepit intellegere quid ig-
noret. et idcirco non uereor notam proditionis
uel leuitatis incurrere, si ea, quae in superiore
tractatu de perfectione orationis disserens dis-
putationi subtraxeram, propalaro, quorum uirtutem uobis in hoc exercitio ac studio conlocatis
etiam sine ministerio nostri sermonis per dei gratiam arbitror fuisse reserandam.

the hands of your experience, getting a sense of certain parts of it here and there. For that reason, I don't think it will take much more work for me to lead you into its innermost chambers, as far as the Lord escorts us, given that you're already basically wandering around the main hall. And there won't be any major obstacle to keep you from scrutinizing the things I'm going to show you.

"You're definitely as close as you can be to knowing something when you pinpoint the question you should be asking. And you're not far from knowledge when you start to recognize what you don't know. So I'm not afraid to risk being seen as indiscreet or easily swayed if I divulge things now that I withheld in our earlier discussion about the perfection of prayer. I think that through God's favor, their power would be revealed to you even without the help of my words, given that you're intensely engaged in this training.

[10.10.1] Quapropter secundum illam insti-
tutionem, quam paruulorum eruditioni pru-
dentissime conparastis (qui alias elementorum
traditionem primam percipere non possunt nec
eorum uel agnoscere lineas uel intrepida manu
queunt describere characteres, quam protypiis
quibusdam et formulis cerae diligenter inpressis
effigies eorum exprimere contemplatione iugi et
cotidiana imitatione consuescant), huius quoque spiritalis theoriae tradenda uobis est formula, ad quam semper tenacissime uestrum
intuitum defigentes uel eandem salubriter uoluere indisrupta iugitate discatis uel sublimiores
intuitus scandere illius usu ac meditatione
possitis.

[10.10.2] haec igitur uobis huius quam quae-
ritis disciplinae atque orationis formula propo-
netur, quam unusquisque monachus ad iugem
dei memoriam tendens incessabili cordis uolutatione meditari expulsa omnium cogitationum

"You very perceptively compared our pedagogy to elementary education. Little kids can't learn the alphabet, make out its shapes, or draw them with a steady hand, unless they keep carefully tracing over models of the letters using templates and models impressed in wax tablets, thinking about them all the time, and practicing every day. In keeping with that idea, I have a model for spiritual contemplation to entrust to you. By keeping it in your sight—always and as tenaciously as possible—you'll learn to keep it turning it over in your mind in perpetual, beneficial motion. And by using it and meditating on it you'll be able to climb to higher vistas.

"So now I'm going to set this device before you, which you've been seeking in your disciplinary practice and prayer. Each and every monk who is striving for an ever-present memory of God should become habituated to meditating on it, going over it continuously with their heart. But first you have to kick out every other

uarietate consuescat, quia nec alias eam ullo
modo poterit retentare, nisi ab omnibus fuerit
corporalibus curis ac sollicitudinibus absolutus.
quae sicut nobis a paucis qui antiquissimorum
patrum residui erant tradita est, ita a nobis quoque non nisi rarissimis ac uere sitientibus inti-
matur. erit itaque ad perpetuam dei memoriam
possidendam haec inseparabiliter proposita
uobis formula pietatis: deus in adiutorium meum
intende: domine ad adiuuandum mihi festina.

[10.10.3] hic namque uersiculus non immerito
de toto scripturarum excerptus est instrumento.
recipit enim omnes adfectus quicumque inferri
humanae possunt naturae et ad omnem statum
atque uniuersos incursus proprie satis et conpetenter aptatur. habet siquidem aduersus uniuersa
discrimina inuocationem dei, habet humilitatem
piae confessionis, habet sollicitudinis ac timoris
perpetui uigilantiam, habet considerationem
fragilitatis suae, exauditionis fiduciam, confi-
dentiam praesentis semper adstantisque praesi-
dii. [10.10.4] qui enim iugiter suum inuocat

kind of thought, because the only way you can keep it up is to disentangle yourself from all your physical and mental preoccupations. Just as it was entrusted to me by the few ancient elders who were still around, I'm sharing it in the same spirit, with only the very few persons who truly thirst for it. So to hold onto a perpetual memory of God, this is the devotional mantra to fix in your mind: 'O God, come to my assistance; O Lord, make haste to help me!'

"This short verse was chosen out of the entirety of the scriptures with good reason. It encompasses every state of mind that can beset human beings, and it is neatly applicable to every situation and all onslaughts. It includes an invocation to God against every possible crisis. It includes the humility of a sincere confession. It includes the alertness that comes from care and constant anxiety. It includes a reflection on one's own weakness, confidence in being heard, and trust that help is always close at hand—[10.10.4] because whoever appeals to their bodyguard

protectorem, certus est eum semper esse praesentem. habet amoris et caritatis ardorem, habet
insidiarum contemplationem inimicorumque
formidinem, quibus perspiciens semet ipsum
die noctuque uallatum confitetur se non posse
sine sui defensoris auxilio liberari.

hic uersiculus omnibus infestatione daemonum laborantibus inexpugnabilis murus est et
inpenctrabilis lurica ac munitissimus clypens.
iste in acedia et anxietate animi conlocatos seu
tristitia uel cogitationibus quibuscumque de-
pressos salutis remedia desperare non patitur,
ostendens illum quem inuocat inspicere iugiter
nostra certamina atque a suis supplicibus non
abesse.

[10.10.5] iste nos in spiritalibus successibus
cordisque laetitia constitutos admonet extolli
penitus non debere nec inflari de prospero statu,

nonstop is certain that he's always there. It includes the burning heat of love and compassion. It includes a cognizance of traps and a fear of enemies. And in perceiving that they are surrounded by them day and night, the speaker admits that they can't be set free without the help of their protector.

"For anyone who is struggling with demonic disturbances, this short verse is an unscalable wall, an impenetrable breastplate, the most fortified shield imaginable. This verse will not allow anyone to lose hope of a lifesaving cure when they find themselves in a state of paralyzing dissatisfaction or mental anxiety, or when they're weighed down by deep sadness or any other kind of thoughts. This verse shows that the one whom it summons is always aware of our struggles and is accessible to his petitioners.

"And when we're flush with spiritual achievements and a celebratory heart, it warns us that we shouldn't gloat or get cocky about our fortunate

quem sine protectore deo retineri non posse tes-
tatur, dum non solum eum semper, sed etiam
uelociter ut sibi auxilietur inplorat.

iste, inquam, uersiculus unicuique nostrum
in qualibet qualitate degenti necessarius et utilis
inuenitur. nam qui se semper atque in omnibus
desiderat adiuuari, manifestat quod non tantum
in rebus duris ac tristibus, sed etiam in secundis
ac laetis pari modo deo egeat adiutore, ut quemadmodum ex illis erui, ita in istis eum faciat
inmorari, in neutro sciens humanam fragilita-
tem sine illius opitulatione subsistere.

[10.10.6] gastrimargiae passione perstringor,
cibos quos heremus ignorat inquiro et in squalida solitudine ingeruntur mihi odores regalium
ferculorum atque ad illorum desideria sentio me
inuitissimum trahi: dicendum proinde mihi est:
deus in adiutorium meum intende: domine ad
adiuuandum mihi festina.

circumstances. We can't maintain them without God acting as a bodyguard, and the verse attests as much by begging God to help out all the time — and quickly!

"Let me be clear: this short verse is useful and essential to each and every one of us regardless of our circumstances. When you always seek help with everything, not just when times are hard or sad but also when they're easygoing and fortunate, you attest to the fact that God is there to assist either way. And it shows you know that human beings, weak as they are, don't subsist in either state without God's support. He's the one who rescues you from trouble and the one who makes the good times last.

"A gluttonous impulse suddenly seizes me. I look around for the sort of food that hermits don't bother with, and in my spare cell the scents of regal meals waft over to me, and I feel like I'm being dragged entirely against my will to crave them. That is when I have to say, 'O God, come to my assistance; O Lord, make haste to help me!'

anticipare horam statutae refectionis instigor seu modum iustae ac solitae parcitatis retinere cum magno cordis mei dolore contendo: cum gemitu mihi est proclamandum: deus in adiutorium meum intende: domine ad adiuuandum mihi festina.

[10.10.7] ieiuniis me ob inpugnationem carnis districtioribus indigentem stomachi prohibct lassitudo scu ucntris ariditas constrictioque deterret: ut effectus meo desiderio tribuatur uel certe ut aestus carnalis concupiscentiae absque temperamento districtioris ieiunii conquiescant, orandum mihi est: deus in adiutorium meum intende: domine ad adiuuandum mihi festina.

accedens ad refectionem hora legitima suggerente perceptionem panis exhorreo atque ab omni esu naturalis necessitatis excludor: cum heiulatu proclamandum est mihi: deus in adiutorium meum intende: domine ad adiuuandum mihi festina.

[10.10.8] uolentem me ob stabilitatem cordis insistere lectioni interpellans capitis prohibet

"Something goads me to start thinking about dinnertime early, or I feel a great pain in my heart that has me straining to stick to the usual moderate portions. I have to call out and lament: 'O God, come to my assistance; O Lord, make haste to help me!'

"A feeling of faintness keeps me from battling my body with stringent fasting, because my stomach is growling. Or maybe it's dryness and cramping in my belly that puts me off. So in order to accomplish what I want, or at the very least to calm my body's agitating urges without fasting more stringently, I have to pray: 'O God, come to my assistance; O Lord, make haste to help me!'

"Then I go to dinner at the right time, and I recoil from the bread, because I'm unable to eat anything I actually need. I have to call out and wail: 'O God, come to my assistance; O Lord, make haste to help me!'

"A headache keeps me from reading to steady my heart: it gets in my way even though I *want*

dolor horaque tertia faciem meam ad sacram paginam somnus adlidit ac deputatum quietis tempus uel transgredi uel praeuenire conpellor, ipsum denique canonicum synaxeos psalmo-rumque modum intercidere me grauissima somni cogit inpressio: similiter proclamandum est mihi: deus in adiutorium meum intende: do-mine ad adiuuandum mihi festina.

sublato ab oculis meis sopore multis me noc-tibus diabolicis insomniis uideo fatigatum omnemque a palpebris meis refectionem noc-turnae quietis exclusam: cum suspiriis orandum est mihi: deus in adiutorium meum intende: do-mine ad adiuuandum mihi festina.

[10.10.9] adhuc me in conluctatione posi-tum uitiorum titillatio carnis repente conpun-git et ad consensum pertrahere dormientem blanda oblectatione conatur: ne ignis alienus exaestuans urat suaue olentes flosculos casti-tatis, clamandum mihi est: deus in adiutorium meum intende: domine ad adiuuandum mihi festina.

to read. Midmorning, drowsiness slams my face down onto the sacred page, and it forces me to oversleep past the allotted time for rest. And eventually the onslaught of a deep sleep moves me to truncate the cycle of psalmody during the liturgy. Again I have to call out: 'O God, come to my assistance; O Lord, make haste to help me!'

"Or say my eyes *don't* close into a deep sleep, and I'm hounded night after night by demonic insomnia, and my eyelids are deprived of a good night's rest. Then I have to pray and sigh: 'O God, come to my assistance; O Lord, make haste to help me!'

"Now, as I struggle against my vulnerabilities, I'm suddenly stung by physical arousal. And while I sleep, it uses seductive turn-ons to try to coerce me into consent. To keep the hostile roaring fire from scorching the sweet-smelling flowers of chastity, I have to call out: 'O God, come to my assistance; O Lord, make haste to help me!'

extincta sentio libidinis incentiua et genitalem
membris meis intepuisse feruorem: ut parta haec
uirtus, immo gratia dei in me diutius uel perpetuo perseueret, intente dicendum est mihi:
deus in adiutorium meum intende: domine ad
adiuuandum mihi festina.

[10.10.10] irae, filargyriae, tristitiae stimulis
inquietor cogorque propositam atque amicam
mihi interrumpere lenitatem: ne in amaritudi-
nem fellis perturbatione furoris abducar, cum
summo mihi gemitu proclamandum est: deus in
adiutorium meum intende: domine ad adiuuandum mihi festina.

acediae, cenodoxiae, superbiae elatione per-
temptor ac de aliorum neglegentia uel tepore
quiddam sibi mens subtili cogitatione blanditur:
ne in me praeualeat haec inimici perniciosa sug-
gestio, cum omni contritione cordis orandum
est mihi: deus in adiutorium meum intende: domine ad adiuuandum mihi festina.

"I sense that the things arousing me have abated and the raging heat in my genitals has cooled: in order for this strength I've gained to persist within me always and forever—with God's support, that is—I have to concentrate and say: 'O God, come to my assistance; O Lord, make haste to help me!'

"I'm agitated by jabs of anger and acquisitiveness and sadness, and I'm shaken out of the mild mood I'd resolved to maintain. To prevent an unsettling rage from dragging me down into bitter resentment, I have to call out and wail: 'O God, come to my assistance; O Lord, make haste to help me!'

"I'm pitted against the pull of boredom, pretentiousness, and pride; and my mind is deluded by the suspicion that other monks are being negligent and indifferent. To keep the enemy's pernicious suggestion from overpowering me, I have to pray with total anguish in my heart: 'O God, come to my assistance; O Lord, make haste to help me!'

[10.10.11] humilitatis et simplicitatis gratiam superbiae tumore deposito iugi conpunctione spiritus adquisiui: ne rursum ueniat mihi pes superbiae et manus peccatoris moueat me grauiusque de uictoriae meae elatione confodiar, totis mihi proclamandum est uiribus: deus in adiutorium meum intende: domine ad adiuuandum mihi festina.

euagationibus animae innumeris ac diuersis et instabilitate cordis exaestuo nec cogitationum disparsiones ualeo cohercere, ipsamque orationem meam fundere absque interpellatione atque phantasmate inanium figurarum sermonumque et actuum retractatione non possum, tantaque me sentio sterilitatis huius ariditate constrictum, ut nullas omnino spiritalium sensuum generationes parturire me sentiam: ut de hoc animi squalore merear liberari, unde me gemitibus multis atque suspiriis expedire non possum, necessarie proclamabo: deus in adiutorium meum intende: domine ad adiuuandum mihi festina.

"Through nonstop spiritual remorse, I've dislodged the tumor of pride and obtained the grace of self-debasement and honesty. To keep the foot of pride from approaching me again, and the hand of the sinner from moving me, and the thrill of my victory from digging me into an even deeper hole, I have to call out with all my might: 'O God, come to my assistance; O Lord, make haste to help me!'

"My soul is bubbling over with countless different distractions, my heart is vacillating, and I'm unable to keep my scattered thoughts under control. I can't pour out that prayer of mine without being interrupted by pointless mental images and inner monologues and rehashed events. I'm so in thrall to these slim pickings that I can't conceive of a single spiritual thought. I can't set myself free with a lot of complaining and moaning, so to earn my liberation from this mental degradation I absolutely have to call out: 'O God, come to my assistance; O Lord, make haste to help me!'

[10.10.12] directionem rursus animae, stabilitatem cogitationum, alacritatem cordis cum ineffabili gaudio et mentis excessu uisitatione sancti spiritus me sentio consecutum, exuberantia quoque spiritalium sensuum redundare reuelationem sacratissimorum intellectuum et antea mihi penitus occultorum repentina domini inlustratione percepi: ut in his merear diutius inmorari, sollicite mihi est frequenterque clamandum: deus in adiutorium meum intende: domine ad adiuuandum mihi festina.

[10.10.13] nocturnis daemonum terroribus circumuallatus exagitor et inmundorum spirituum phantasmatibus inquietor, spes ipsa mihi salutis ac uitae trepidationis horrore subtrahitur: ad salutarem uersiculi huius portum confugiens totis uiribus exclamabo: deus in adiutorium meum intende: domine ad adiuuandum mihi festina.

"Thanks to an appearance from the Holy Spirit, I feel my soul has found its footing again, my thoughts have settled, and my heart is alert. My joy is inexpressible, and my mind is transported. I'm overflowing with a superabundance of spiritual perceptions, and thanks to a sudden inspiration from the Lord, the most hallowed forms of knowledge that were once totally hidden from me have been uncovered, and I understand them. To earn more time to linger here, I have to cry out anxiously and repeatedly: 'O God, come to my assistance; O Lord, make haste to help me!'

"I'm being harassed by demonic nightmares that surround me on all sides. I'm disturbed by images of filthy spirits. And hope itself—of being saved, of being alive—is dragged away from me through sheer terror. Taking refuge in that lifesaving harbor of this brief verse, I will exclaim with all my might: 'O God, come to my assistance; O Lord, make haste to help me!'

rursus cum fuero consolatione domini repa-
ratus et ipsius animatus aduentu uelut innumeris
angelorum milibus me sensero circumsaeptum,
ita ut eorum, quos morte grauius antea tremesce-
bam et quorum tactum, immo uiciniam horrore
mentis et corporis sentiebam, repente congres-
sus expetere audeam ac prouocare conflictus: ut
in me constantiae huius uigor per dei gratiam
diutius inmoretur, totis mihi est uiribus proclamandum: deus in adiutorium meum intende:
domine ad adiuuandum mihi festina.

[10.10.14] huius igitur uersiculi oratio in adu-
ersis ut eruamur, in prosperis ut seruemur nec
extollamur incessabili iugitate fundenda est.
huius, inquam, uersiculi meditatio in tuo pec-
tore indisrupta uoluatur. hunc in opere quolibet
seu ministerio uel itinere constitutus decantare
non desinas. hunc et dormiens et reficiens et in
ultimis naturae necessitatibus meditare. haec

"Then once I've recovered in the comfort of the Lord and been revived by his approach, I feel as though thousands and thousands of angels are encircling me. As a result, I suddenly have the courage to seek out and face the demons I feared worse than death until just now—the demons whose touch felt so close it used to make my mind and body quake. I challenge them to fight, and, to maintain this stamina for a while longer with God's support, I have to call out with all my might: 'O God, come to my assistance; O Lord, make haste to help me!'

"And so, we should pour out this brief verse in nonstop constant prayer—to be rescued when we're embattled, and to be preserved when we're flourishing without it going to our heads. I'll say it again: you should recite this brief verse in an unbroken cycle in your breast. Whether you're working, or performing some task, or traveling, you should never stop chanting it. You should recite it when you're sleeping and eating and going to the bathroom. This

uolutatio cordis uelut formula tibi salutaris effecta non solum inlaesum ab omni daemonum incursione custodiet, sed etiam cunctis te uitiis terrenae contagionis expurgans ad illas inuisibiles theorias caelestesque perducet atque ad illum ineffabilem ac perpaucis expertum prouehet orationis ardorem.

[10.10.15] hunc uersiculum meditanti tibi somnus inrepat, donec incessabili eius exercitatione formatus etiam per soporem eum decantare consuescas. hic tibi expergefacto primus occurrat, iste euigilantis cogitationes anticipet uniuersas, iste te de tuo surgentem cubili curuationi genuum tradat atque illinc deinceps ad omne opus actusque deducat, hic te omni tempore prosequatur. hunc meditaberis secundum praecepta legislatoris sedens in domo et ambulans in itinere, dormiens atque consurgens. hunc

perpetual motion of the heart will become a lifesaving formula for you. Not only will it keep you unharmed from any demonic attack. It will also purge you of all the contaminating weaknesses of everyday life. It will guide you toward those unseen celestial contemplations. And it will transport you to that inexpressible fiery prayer that very few people experience.

"May you nod off while you're meditating on this verse, until you've become so conditioned to the constant practice of it that you chant it even while you're fast asleep. May it be the first thing to greet you when you wake up. May it anticipate all the thoughts you'll have when you're awake. May it usher you to kneel when you rise from your bed, and then from there, may it conduct you through all your deeds and affairs. May it always be at your side. In accordance with the Lawgiver's commands, you will meditate on this verse when you sit in your house, and when you walk by the way, and when you lie down, and when you rise up. You will

scribes in limine et ianuis oris tui, hunc in parieti-
bus domus tuae ac penetralibus tui pectoris con-
locabis, ita ut haec ad orationem procumbenti
sit tibi adclinis decantatio et exinde consurgenti
atque ad omnes usus uitae necessarios incedenti
fiat erecta et iugis oratio.

[10.11.1] Istam, istam mens indesinenter formulam teneat, donec usu eius incessabili et iugi
meditatione firmata cunctarum cogitationum
diuitias amplasque substantias abiciat ac refutet,
atque ita uersiculi huius paupertate constricta
ad illam euangelicam beatitudinem, quae inter
ceteras beatitudines primatum tenet, prona facilitate perueniat. beati enim inquit pauperes
spiritu, quoniam ipsorum est regnum caelorum.
et ita quis per istiusmodi paupertatem egregius
pauper exsistens illud propheticum inplebit
eloquium: pauper et inops laudabit nomen
domini.

write it over your threshold, and on the doors of your mouth. You will place it on the walls of your house, and in the innermost chambers of your breast. That way, this chant will be with you when you bow to pray, and then again when you rise. And as you go about the obligatory business of everyday life, may your prayer be ever attentive.

"The mind should maintain its hold on this mantra without letting up, through constant use and nonstop and intense meditation, until it has tossed out and rejected the riches and vast resources of all its thoughts. In this way the mind will become bound up in the poverty of this verse and will all the more easily reach that state of bliss that holds pride of place among the others. 'Blessed are the poor in spirit,' he says, 'for theirs is the kingdom of heaven.' So whoever excels as a poor person in this kind of poverty will fulfill that prophetic utterance: 'The poor and the needy shall praise the name of the Lord.'"

[10.12] GERMANVS: Non solum nobis traditionem spiritalis huius quam poposcimus disciplinae, sed ipsam plane perfectionem satis
aperte atque dilucide putamus expressam. quid
enim potest esse perfectius quidue sublimius
quam dei memoriam tam conpendiosa meditatione conplecti atque unius uersiculi uolutatione
a cunctis uisibilium terminis emigrare et quodammodo affectus orationum cunctarum breui
sermone concludere?

et idcirco unum quod superest adhuc nobis
precamur exponi, quemadmodum hunc eundem
uersiculum quem nobis uice formulae tradidisti
stabiliter retinere possimus, ut sicut per dei gratiam sumus a saecularium cogitationum ineptiis liberati, ita spiritales quasque inmobiliter
retentemus.

[10.13.1] Cum enim capitulum cuiuslibet
psalmi mens nostra conceperit, insensibiliter eo
subtracto ad alterius scripturae textum nesciens

A MANTRA

Germanus said: "Not only have you shared with us the spiritual discipline we were begging for. We also think you've clearly and straightforwardly described the perfect execution of it. After all, what could be a more elevated achievement than to encompass the memory of God with such a brief form of meditation? To leave the realm of the visible world behind by repeating a single short verse? To somehow encapsulate the moods of all possible prayers with this small phrase?

"So now there's only one final thing we're hoping you'll explain to us. This verse you've given us as a mantra: how can we hold on to it so steadily that (insofar as God grants it) we're set free from irrelevant thoughts and at the same time can hold tight to spiritual ones without letting go?

"See, whenever we think of a section of some psalm, that bit gets plowed over for some reason, and the mind is sent rolling into a passage

stupensque deuoluitur. cumque illud in semet ipsa coeperit uolutare, necdum illo ad integrum uentilato oborta alterius testimonii memoria meditationem materiae prioris excludit. de hac quoque ad alteram subintrante alia meditatione transfertur, et ita animus semper de psalmo rotatus ad psalmum, de euangelii textu ad apostoli transiliens lectionem, de hac quoque ad prophetica deuolutus eloquia et exinde ad quasdam spiritales delatus historias per omne scripturarum corpus instabilis uagusque iactatur, nihil pro arbitrio suo praeualens uel abicere uel tenere nec pleno quicquam iudicio et examinatione finire, palpator tantummodo spiritalium sensuum ac degustator, non generator nec possessor effectus.

from another part of scripture, unaware and clueless about what's happening. And when it starts to loop through *that* passage within itself, it interrupts its reflection on that material—though it wasn't done with it yet—with a memory that sprang up from some other prompt. From there it's relocated to something else, thanks to yet another intrusive association, and that's how it goes: the mind is always tossed around, unstable and meandering, spinning from psalm to psalm, jumping from a gospel text to a reading of the apostle, tumbling from there into the prophetic books, only to be carried off into haphazard spots throughout the scriptural narratives, failing (despite its ability to make decisions) to jettison or grip onto anything with any real conviction, or even to set some boundaries after giving it some thought, so that in the end it only gets a touch or taste of spiritual sensations rather than producing or controlling what it experiences![41]

[10.13.2] atque ita mens mobilis semper ac uaga in tempore quoque synaxeos uelut ebria per diuersa distrahitur, nullum officium conpetenter exsoluens. uerbi gratia cum orat, psalmum aut aliquam recolit lectionem. cum decantat, aliud quid meditatur quam textus ipsius continet psalmi. cum lectionem recitat, faciendum aliquid uoluit factumue reminiscitur. atque in hunc modum nihil disciplinate nec oportune recipiens uel dimittens uelut fortuitis agi uidetur incursibus, retinendi ea quibus delectatur uel inmorandi eis non habens potestatem.

[10.13.3] necessarium ergo nobis est prae omnibus nosse quemadmodum haec spiritalia conpetenter explere possimus officia uel certe hunc eundem uersiculum, quem nobis uice formulae tradidisti, inmobiliter custodire, ut omnium

"And so it goes: the mind is always moving and meandering, and it's torn apart in different directions like it's drunk, even during the liturgy, and in the process it doesn't perform any of its functions adequately. While it prays, for example, it's recalling a psalm or something else it has read. While it chants, it's thinking about something besides what the psalm text says. While it recites a reading, it's imagining what it wants to do or what it wishes it had done instead. And when it's behaving like that, it doesn't accept or reject any idea in a controlled or useful way. It seems to get pushed around by random distractions, and it doesn't even have the power to hold onto or stick with the things it finds entertaining!

"That's why more than anything else, we need to know how we can possibly fulfill our spiritual duties as we're supposed to, or at least how we can stay unwaveringly alert to the short verse that you gave us to use as a mantra. That

sensuum ortus ac fines non in sua uolubilitate fluctuent, sed in nostra dicione consistant.

[10.14.1] ISAAC: Licet pridem super hac re disputantibus nobis de orationis statu, quantum reor, sit sufficienter expressum, tamen quia nobis haec eadem poscitis iterari, de confirmatione cordis breuiter intimabo. tria sunt quae uagam mentem stabilem faciunt, uigiliae, meditatio et oratio, quarum adsiduitas et iugis intentio conferunt animae stabilem firmitatem.

[10.14.2] quae tamen alias nullo modo poterit adprehendi, nisi per operis non filargyriae, sed sacris coenobii usibus dedicati infatigabilem iugitatem omnes omnino sollicitudines et curae uitae praesentis prius fuerint abdicatae, ut ita illud apostolicum mandatum: sine intermissione orate possimus inplere. perparum namque orat, quisquis illo tantum tempore quo genua flectuntur

way, all our conscious perceptions won't keep getting sucked in or spit out of this whirlpool. Instead they'll stand still, under our control."

Isaac said: "I feel like I said enough about this topic earlier, when we were discussing the approach to prayer. But since you're asking me to repeat the same thing again, I'll briefly address the subject of how to make the heart stronger. There are three things that stabilize a meandering mind: keeping vigil at night, reciting and reflecting on scripture, and praying. The persistence and constant mental stretch of these practices brings a steady strength to the soul.

"But there's no way to attain this state of mind unless we're tirelessly and constantly dedicated to our work—not profit-obsessed work, but our sacred monastic practices. All our concerns and worries about life in the present should be totally swept away, so we might be able to fulfill the apostolic command to pray without ceasing. Whoever makes a habit of praying only when they kneel down doesn't really pray very

orare consueuit. numquam uero orat, quisquis etiam flexis genibus euagatione cordis qualicumque distrahitur. et idcirco quales orantes uolumus inueniri, tales nos esse oportet ante tempus orandi. necesse est enim mentem in tempore supplicationis suae de statu praecedente formari illisque eam cogitationibus orantem uel ad caelestia sublimari uel ad terrena demergi, quibus ante orationem fuerit inmorata.

[10.14.3] Huc usque abbas Isaac adtonitis nobis secundam conlationem de orationis qualitate digessit. cuius doctrinam super illius praedicti uersiculi meditatione, quam uelut informationis loco ab incipientibus tradiderat retinendam, admirantes admodum et excolere tenacissime cupientes, utpote quam conpendiosam ac facilem credebamus, difficiliorem satis ad obseruandum

much. Actually, even when it comes to praying while you're kneeling, you're not praying at all if you're being dragged around wherever your heart wanders. For that reason, we should be the sort of person that we want to be in prayer *before* it's time to pray. After all, our state of mind during prayer is unavoidably shaped by the situation prior to that moment. So depending on where the mind's thoughts were lingering beforehand, when it goes to pray it will be either vaulted up to the heavens or plunged down to earth."

We were floored by the time Abba Isaac finished our second consultation about how to pray. He had entrusted us with his lesson about meditating on that one little verse, which beginners were supposed to keep in mind as source of guidance. We were totally amazed and wanted nothing more than to become experts at it, because we were sure that what he'd taught us was short and easy. But we realized, after

experti sumus quam illud studium nostrum, quo solebamus antea per omne scripturarum corpus absque ullius perseuerantiae uinculo uaria passim meditatione discurrere.

constat igitur neminem prorsus ob inperitiam litterarum a perfectione cordis excludi nec rusticitatem obesse ad capessendam cordis atque animae puritatem, quae conpendiosissime adiacet cunctis, si modo sanam et integram mentis intentionem iugi ad deum uersiculi huius meditatione seruauerint.

trying it out, that it was harder than the effort we used to spend zigzagging across all the scriptures without being tethered to anything for long.

Point taken: nobody is excluded from perfecting their heart because they aren't well educated. Growing up country doesn't prevent anyone from pursuing clarity of the heart and soul, either. These opportunities are close within reach of everybody, if they maintain a good strong mental stretch out to God while constantly reciting and reflecting on this short verse.

[14.10.1] Festinandum igitur tibi est, si ad ueram scripturarum uis scientiam peruenire, ut humilitatem cordis inmobilem primitus consequaris, quae te non ad illam quae inflat, sed ad eam quae inluminat scientiam caritatis consummatione perducat. inpossibile namque est inmundam mentem donum scientiae spiritalis adipisci. et idcirco omni cautione deuita, ne tibi per studium lectionis non scientiae lumen nec illa perpetua quae per inluminationem doctrinae promittitur gloria, sed instrumenta perditionis de adrogantiae uanitate nascantur.

[14.10.2] deinde hoc tibi est omnimodis enitendum, ut expulsa omni sollicitudine et cogitatione

MEMORIES

Cassian and Germanus Consult Abba Nesteros, an Anchorite near Panephysis

Nesteros said: "If you want to arrive at the true knowledge of the scriptures, the first thing you need to do is start pursuing steady self-abasement in your heart right away. That humility will make you compassionate, and in doing so it will lead you to knowledge that enlightens you rather than inflates you. After all, it's impossible for a muddled mind to receive the gift of insight into the meanings of scripture.[42] You need take every precaution to avoid a situation in which your serious reading causes your own downfall because you've become pointlessly conceited—instead of generating luminous knowledge and the eternal glory that educational enlightenment can offer.

"Then, after you've driven out every concern and mundane thought, you need to devote all

terrena adsiduum te ac potius iugem sacrae
praebeas lectioni, donec continua meditatio in-
buat mentem tuam et quasi in similitudinem sui
formet, arcam quodammodo ex ea faciens testamenti, habentem scilicet in se duas tabulas
lapideas, id est duplicis instrumenti perpetuam
firmitatem: urnam quoque auream, hoc est memoriam puram atque sinceram, quae recondi-
tum in se manna perpetua tenacitate conseruet,
spiritalium scilicet sensuum et angelici illius
panis perennem caelestemque dulcedinem: nec
non etiam uirgam Aaron, id est summi uerique
pontificis nostri Iesu Christi salutare uexillum,
inmortalis memoriae semper uiriditate fronde-
scens. [14.10.3] haec namque est uirga quae
posteaquam de Iesse radice succisa est uiuacius
mortificata reuirescit.

haec autem omnia duobus Cherubin, id est
historicae et spiritalis scientiae plenitudine pro-
tegentur. Cherubin enim interpretatur scientiae

your energy to sacred reading, and to do it con-
tinually—or better, nonstop!—until that constant recitation and reflection saturates your
mind and shapes it into a kind of likeness of
itself. Think of it as transforming your mind
into the Ark of the Covenant, containing two
stone tablets signifying the eternal endurance of
the two testamentary records, a golden vessel
signifying a clear and sound memory that perfectly preserves manna within it forever (the
manna representing the everlasting heavenly
sweetness of that bread of the angels: the spiritual perceptions), and the rod of Aaron leafing
with the evergreen of undying memory, signifying the salvific banner of our true and highest
priest, Jesus Christ. This rod is in fact the branch
that had been cut away from the root of Jesse,
only to grow back even more vigorously after
it was killed off.

"All these objects are guarded by two cherubim, signifying the full extent of historical and
spiritual knowledge,[43] for the cherubim are

multitudo: quae propitiatorium dei, id est pla-
ciditatem pectoris tui iugiter protegent et a cunctis
spiritalium nequitiarum incursibus obum-
brabunt. et ita mens tua non solum in arcam
diuini testamenti, uerum etiam in regnum sac-
erdotale prouecta per indissolubilem puritatis
affectum quodammodo absorta spiritalibus dis-
ciplinis illud inplebit pontificale mandatum,
quod a legislatore ita praccipitur: et de sanctis
non egredietur, ne polluat sanctuarium dei, id
est cor suum, in quo iugiter habitaturum se dominus repromittit dicens: inhabitabo in eis et
inter illos ambulabo.

[14.10.4] quamobrem diligenter memoriae
conmendanda est et incessabiliter recensenda
sacrarum series scripturarum. haec etenim meditationis iugitas duplicem nobis conferet fructum: primum quod, dum in legendis ac parandis
lectionibus occupatur mentis intentio, necesse
est ut nullis noxiarum cogitationum laqueis

interpreted to mean all that is known. They keep constant watch over God's sanctuary—that stillness in your breast—and they will protect you from every demonic onslaught. In this way, your mind will be transported, not just to the Ark of the Divine Covenant, but even to the priestly kingdom. Through an unshakeable feeling of tranquility it becomes, in a way, swallowed up in spiritual forms of conduct, and it fulfills that priestly command issued by the Lawmaker: 'Neither shall he go out of the holy places, lest he defile the sanctuary of his God'—meaning his heart, where the Lord promised he would reside perpetually. As he said, 'I will dwell in them and walk among them.'

"That's why we should resolutely commit the whole series of the sacred scriptures to memory and go over them all the time. This nonstop meditation is doubly beneficial. First, while the mind's attention is engrossed in reading and internalizing texts, there's no way for toxic thoughts to entrap it. Second, while we're working

captiuetur: deinde quod ea, quae creberrima repetitione percursa, dum memoriae tradere laboramus, intellegere id temporis obligata mente non
quiuimus, postea ab omnium actuum ac uisio-
num inlecebris absoluti praecipueque nocturna
meditatione taciti reuoluentes clarius intuemur,
ita ut occultissimorum sensuum, quos ne tenui
quidem uigilantes opinatione percepimus, quies-
centibus nobis et uelut soporis stupore demersis
intellegentia reueletur.

[14.11.1] Crescente autem per hoc studium
innouatione mentis nostrae etiam scripturarum
facies incipiet innouari, et sacratioris intellegent-
iae pulchritudo quodammodo cum proficiente
proficiet. pro capacitate enim humanorum sensuum earum quoque species coaptatur et uel
terrena carnalibus uel diuina spiritalibus adpar-
ebit, ita ut hi, quibus antea uidebatur crassis quibusdam nebulis inuoluta, nec subtilitatem eius
deprehendere nec fulgorem ualeant sustinere.

hard to memorize certain passages by going over and over them, we can't understand them in the moment because our mind is so engaged—but after we've been cut loose from the pull of things that keep happening and popping up, especially at night when we've fallen silent in meditation and keep turning the scriptures over in our minds, we see things so much more clearly. It's when we are still, just as if we're plunged deep in sleep, that we perceive the things that were most obscure to us, things that we barely understood when we were wide awake.

"But there is more. As our mind is gradually remade through this sustained effort, the shape of the scriptures begins to be remade, too, and it's as if the beauty born of this more sacred perceptiveness grows as we grow. How the scriptures look depends on what the human senses are capable of: to physical modes of perception they appear to be earthly, and to spiritual modes they appear to be divine. As a result, people who see the scriptures cloaked in a dense

sed ut hoc ipsum quod adstruere nitimur aliquo clarius pandatur exemplo, unum legis tes-
timonium protulisse sufficiat, per quod etiam
omnia praecepta caelestia secundum mensuram
status nostri ad omne hominum genus probe-
mus extendi. [14.11.2] scriptum est in lege: non
fornicaberis. hoc ab homine carnalium adhuc
obscenitatum passionibus obligato secundum
simplicem litterae sonum salubriter custoditur.
ab eo autem qui iam ab hac actione lutulenta et
inpuro discessit affectu necesse est id ipsum spir-
italiter obseruari, ut scilicet non solum a caeri-
moniis idolorum, sed etiam ab omni superstitione
gentilium et auguriorum atque ominum omni-
umque signorum et dierum ac temporum ob-
seruatione discedat, uel certe ne quorundam
uerborum aut nominum coniecturis, quae sin-
ceritatem fidei nostrae polluunt, inplicetur.

fog can't make out their fine features or bask in their brightness.

"By way of example, it's enough to proffer one piece of evidence from the Law to help clarify what we're trying to lay out here. With it we can prove that all heavenly teachings speak to every human being, commensurate with where we stand. In the Law it is written: 'Thou shalt not commit adultery.' A person who is still prone to inappropriate sexual impulses observes this literally, for their own good. But a person who has already sworn off those dirty behaviors and filthy mentality needs to heed the *spiritual* sense of the same commandment. This means distancing oneself from idolatrous rituals, and from all the superstitions of the pagans and soothsayers, and from prognostications and the astrological charting of signs and days and phases. It also means not getting caught up in telling fortunes based on certain words and terms—a practice that defiles the integrity of our faith."[44]

[14.11.5] . . . hanc etiam qui potuerit declinare, caueat ne subtiliore peccato in fornicationis ui- tium conlabatur, quae scilicet in cogitationum peruagatione consistit, quia omnis cogitatio non solum turpis, sed etiam otiosa et a deo quantu- lumcumque discedens a perfecto uiro inmundis- sima fornicatio deputatur.

[14.12] Ad haec ego occulta primum conpunc- tione permotus ac deinde grauiter ingemescens: haec, inquam, omnia quae copiosissime diges- sisti maiora mihi intulerunt desperationis aug- menta quam hactenus sustinebam: quippe cui praeter illas generales animae captiuitates, qui- bus non dubito infirmos quosque pulsari extrin- secus, speciale inpedimentum salutis accedit per illam quam tenuiter uideor adtigisse notitiam lit- terarum, in qua me ita uel instantia paedagogi

LATER IN THE CONVERSATION WITH NESTEROS

[Nesteros went on:] "And even a person who is able to avoid such scenarios should take care not to lapse into the failure of fornication through subtler sins—distracted thoughts, in other words—because from the point of view of a perfect man, every disgusting thought, every pointless thought, every thought that distances itself from God even the tiniest bit, is an utterly obscene act of fornication."

[Cassian.] When I heard these things, I was deeply moved at first by an inner sting of remorse, and then I began to moan. I said, "Everything you've so thoroughly laid out here makes me feel even more at a loss than I already was. Because even leaving aside those common entrapments of the soul, which I'm certain keep battering vulnerable people from the outside in, there is a particular obstacle to salvation in my way. And that is my passing acquaintance with literature. I was steeped in those texts thanks to

uel continuae lectionis macerauit intentio, ut nunc mens mea poeticis illis uelut infecta carminibus illas fabularum nugas historiasque bellorum, quibus a paruulo primis studiorum inbuta est rudimentis, orationis etiam tempore meditetur, psallentique uel pro peccatorum indulgentia supplicanti aut inpudens poematum memoria suggeratur aut quasi bellantium heroum ante oculos imago uersetur, taliumque me phantasmatum imaginatio semper inludens ita mentem meam ad supernos intuitus adspirare non patitur, ut cotidianis fletibus non possit expelli.

[14.13.1] NESTEROS: De hac ipsa re, unde tibi purgationis maxima nascitur desperatio, citum satis atque efficax remedium poterit oboriri, si eandem diligentiam atque instantiam, quam te in illis saecularibus studiis habuisse dixisti, ad spiritalium scripturarum uolueris lectionem meditationemque transferre. necesse est enim mentem tuam tamdiu illis carminibus

the insistence of my teacher and the attention I gave to bouts of reading, so now it's like my mind is tainted by that poetry. Even when it's time to pray, my mind meditates on the silly stories and military histories that it soaked up back when I was a little boy in elementary school.[45] And when I'm singing psalms or making entreaties for my sins to be pardoned, an insolent memory from those poems will pop up, or heroes will start battling it out before my eyes. These mental images are always toying with me, keeping my mind from reaching more celestial vistas, and I can't even drive them off through my daily practice of weeping."

Nesteros said: "This problem may have made you lose hope of ever getting rid of it, but there is a quick and effective cure that can be developed. You only need to be willing to apply the same dedication and tenacity to reading and meditating on spiritual writings that you said you'd kept up in your nonreligious studies. The time that your mind spent occupied by those poems:

occupari, quamdiu sibi alia quae intra semet ipsam recolat simili studio et adsiduitate conquirat ac pro illis infructuosis atque terrenis spiritalia ac diuina parturiat.

[14.13.2] quae cum profunde alteque conceperit atque in illis fuerit enutrita, uel expelli priores sensim poterunt uel penitus aboleri. uacare enim cunctis cogitationibus humana mens non potest, et ideo quamdiu spiritalibus studiis non fuerit occupata, necesse est eam illis quae pridem didicit inplicari. quamdiu enim non habuerit quo recurrat et indefessos exerceat motus, necesse est ut ad illa quibus ab infantia inbuta est conlabatur eaque semper reuoluat quae longo usu ac meditatione concepit.

[14.13.3] ut ergo haec in te scientia spiritalis perpetua soliditate roboretur nec ea iam temporarie perfruaris sicut illi qui eam non suo studio, sed aliena relatione contingunt et uelut aërio ut

that's how long it will have to spend tending a new crop of things within itself, carrying out the work with the same effort and persistence, and producing spiritual and divine thoughts instead of those unproductive earthly ones.

"And when the mind is schooled in *those* subjects and starts thinking deeply and soaringly, it can gradually drive out that older material or utterly destroy it. After all, it's impossible for the human mind to empty itself of all thoughts. So if it isn't spending much time on spiritual activities, it's inevitably going to get caught up in things it learned a long time ago. When it doesn't have a place to go to keep up its inexhaustible exercises, it inevitably falls back on what it absorbed when it was young, and it keeps repeating the things it has practiced and thought about for ages.

"Consequently, this scriptural knowledge should be strengthened into an enduringly solid state in you. It should no longer be something you enjoy only fleetingly, like other people who grasp it only vicariously rather than through

ita dixerim odore percipiunt, sed ut sensibus tuis inuiscerata quodammodo et perspecta atque palpata condatur, illud omni obseruantia custodire te conuenit, ut etiamsi ea quae optime nosti forte audieris in conlatione proferri, non ex hoc quod tibi iam nota sint aspernanter fastidioseque suscipias, sed ea cordi tuo illa auiditate conmendes, qua debent desiderabilia salutis uerba uel auribus nostris indesinenter infundi uel de nostro iugiter ore proferri.

[14.13.4] quamuis enim adhibeatur sanctarum rerum crebra narratio, numquam tamen animae sitim uerae scientiae sustinenti satietas generabit horrorem, sed ea cotidie uelut noua ac desiderata suscipiens quanto frequentius hauserit, tanto auidius uel audiet uel loquetur et confirmationem potius perceptae scientiae ex eorum repetitione quam ullum ex frequenti capiet conlatione

their own efforts: they experience it like a waft-
ing scent, I'd say. But for you, it should be
grounded in your senses as if you'd seen and
touched and digested it. And to accomplish all of
this, you should concentrate completely on re-
specting the following principle: that even when
it's the case that someone is talking about things
you already know really well, you shouldn't
treat what you already know as unappetizing or
unappealing. Instead you should entrust that in-
formation to your heart with the same hunger
we're supposed to feel when the choice words of
salvation are poured unceasingly into our ears
and uttered nonstop by our mouth.

"No matter how often a discussion of sacred
subjects comes up, a person whose soul thirsts
for true knowledge will never be put off or
sated. Every day they treat it like it's a brand-
new thing they've been waiting for. The more
often they drink it in, the more voraciously they
listen and talk. And rather than get bored by a
conversation they have repeatedly, the repetition

fastidium. euidens namque est tepidae ac super-
bae mentis indicium, si uerborum salutarium
medicinam quamuis studio nimiae adsiduitatis
ingestam fastidiose neglegenterque suscipiat:
anima enim quae in satietate est fauis inludit, animae autem egenti etiam amara dulcia uidentur.

[14.13.5] si itaque haec diligenter excepta et
in recessu mentis condita atque indicta fuerint
taciturnitate signata, postea ut uina quaedam
suaue olentia et laetificantia cor hominis, cum
sensuum canitie et patientiae fuerint uetustate
decocta, cum magna sui fragrantia de uase tui
pectoris proferentur et tamquam perennis fons
de experientiae uenis et inriguis uirtutum meati-
bus redundabunt fluentaque continua uelut de
quadam abysso tui cordis effundent.

instead verifies the knowledge they've already acquired. It's a clear sign that a mind is lukewarm and arrogant if it's careless or squeamish about taking the medicine of lifesaving words, no matter how energetic the efforts are to prescribe it for them. A soul in plenitude scorns honeycombs, but to the needy soul even bitter things appear sweet.

"If a person handles these discussions carefully, sets them in the back of the mind, and stores them in a specially designated silent cellar, the heart will later emerge like a sweetly fragrant wine that maketh glad the heart of man. Once they have been aged by mature perspective and long-standing endurance, they will emerge from the bottle of your breast full of aroma. And like a never-ending fountain they will overflow through the veins of your expertise and the arteries of your strength in a constant course, as if they were pouring out of some bottomless sea in your heart."

[23.5.7] . . . inpossibile est enim etiam menti, quae tam crebris distenditur curis, tam uariis, tam molestis angoribus praepeditur, diuino frui semper intuitu. quod enim tam pertinax sanctorum studium, quod tam arduum potest esse propositum, cui non aliquando ille uersutus insidiator inludat?

[23.5.8] quis ita solitudinis secreta sectatus est et uniuersorum mortalium consortia declinauit, ut numquam cogitationibus superfluis laboretur et intuitu rerum uel occupatione actuum terrenorum ab illa quae uere sola et bona est dei contemplatione decideret? quis tantum spiritus umquam potuit retinere feruorem, ut non interdum lubricis cogitationibus ab ipsa quoque

SLIP-UPS

Cassian and Germanus Consult
Abba Theonas of Scetis

Theonas said: "It is impossible for the mind to partake of a vision of the divine at all times, because it's pulled in all directions by so many worries and entangled in such varied and annoying problems. Are there even any saints who undertake training that is *so* tenacious, or have intentions that are *so* rigorous, that the shrewd manipulator won't sometimes toy with them?

"And is there anyone who has gone into hiding and avoided the company of all other human beings who is *never* afflicted by pointless thoughts? Whose contemplation of God is so exclusive and wholesome that they stop picturing and engaging with earthly things entirely? Is there anyone who can ever maintain such an intense spiritual heat that they don't suddenly

orationis intentione translatus repente de cae-
lestibus ad terrena conrueret? quis nostrum, ut
cetera peruagationum tempora praetermittam,
non illo etiam momento, quo deo supplicans ad
sublimia erigit mentem, quodam stupore conlap-
sus etiam per id uel inuitus offendat, per quod
sperabat ueniam delictorum?

[23.5.9] quis, inquam, tam exertus ac uigilans
est, ut dum psalmum deo canit numquam ab
scripturae sensu eius animus abducatur? quis tam
familiaris deo tamque coniunctus, qui apostolicum illud imperium, quo sine intermissione
orare nos praecipit, uel uno die se gaudeat
exsecutum?

quae licet omnia nonnullis, qui sunt crassi-
oribus uitiis inuoluti, leuia atque a peccato paene
aliena uideantur, scientibus tamen perfectionis
bonum etiam minimarum rerum multitudo
grauissima est.

backslide from the heavens to the earth because their attention in prayer has been hijacked by slippery thoughts? And leaving aside other instances of distraction, is there anyone among us who has not checked out at the very moment when we're making entreaties to God and lifting our mind to the heights—and end up unintentionally offending him in our attempt to obtain pardon for our faults!?

"I could go on. Is there anyone who is so driven and alert that when they're chanting a psalm to God their mind is never drawn away from their focus on scripture? Is there anyone who is on such friendly terms with God, who is so connected with him, that they can actually say that they followed the apostle's command to us to pray without ceasing for one whole day?

Sure, to some people (people who are wrapped up in much more glaring flaws), all of this may seem insignificant and basically irrelevant to the subject of sin. But to people who know how good perfection is, the agglomeration of even

[23.9.1] Recte igitur sanctos, qui memoriam dei stabiliter retinentes quasi per extentas in sublime lineas suspenso feruntur incessu, schoenobatis, quos uulgo funambulos uocant, dixerim conparandos, qui summam suae salutis ac uitae in angustissimo funiculi illius tramite conlocantes atrocissimam se mortem protinus incursuros esse non ambigunt, si uel exigua pes eorum titubatione deuiauerit aut modum illius salutaris directionis excesserit.

[23.9.2] qui dum arte mirifica aërios gressus per inania moliuntur, si illam angustiorem uestigio semitam non cauta atque sollicita moderatione seruauerint, terra, quae omnibus uelut naturalis est basis et solidissimum cunctis ac tutissimum fundamentum, fit illis praesens ac manifesta pernicies, non quia illius natura mutetur,

the most minor things weighs on them very heavily."

Later in the Conversation with Theonas

"The saints who keep a steady hold on their memory of God, like they're forever walking aloft on cables stretched out to the skies: I'd say it's worth comparing them to funambulists or tightrope walkers. They stake their life and salvation on the incomparably narrow path of that razor-thin wire, and they know all too well that they'll fall to a grisly death the instant they waver and take a single misstep or wrong turn.

"And as the practitioners of this marvelous craft undertake their aerial climb through the void, they must mind that narrow path with sure footing and careful control. Otherwise, the ground—which for everyone else is a natural baseline, a firm and reassuring foundation—spells obvious and immediate extinction for them, not

sed quia illi ad eam praecipiti carnis pondere delabuntur. ita etiam indefessa illa dei bonitas inmutabilisque substantia ipsa quidem neminem laedit, sed nos declinando a summis atque ad ima tendendo nobis ipsi consciscimus mortem, immo ipsa declinatio mors efficitur declinanti.

[23.9.3] uae enim inquit eis, quoniam recesserunt a me: uastabuntur, quoniam praeuaricati sunt in me, et iterum: uae eis cum recessero ab eis. arguet namque te malitia tua, et auersio tua increpabit te. scito, et uide quam malum et amarum est reliquisse te dominum deum tuum. funiculis namque peccatorum suroum unusquisque constringitur. ad quos satis conpetenter a domino increpatio illa dirigitur: ecce, inquit, omnes uos accendentes ignem accincti flammis, ambulate in lumine ignis uestri, et in flammis, quas succendistis, et iterum qui incendit, inquit, malitiam, peribit ab ea.

because the nature of the ground changes but because the weight of their bodies would bring them smashing down into it. The same is true of the tireless goodness of God and his unchanging essence itself. They do not harm anyone. We inflict death on ourselves, by turning away from the heights toward the depths. The fall itself is deadly.

"'Woe unto them!' he says, 'for they have fled from me: destruction unto them! because they have transgressed against me.' And elsewhere: 'Woe to them when I depart from them!' Thy backslidings shall reprove thee; know therefore and see that it is an evil thing and bitter, that thou hast forsaken the Lord thy God. Each one is bound by the ropes of his own sins. The objects of the Lord's rebuke are quite appropriately singled out in this passage: 'Behold, all ye that kindle a fire, that compass yourselves about with sparks: walk in the light of your fire, and in the sparks that ye have kindled.' And here, too: 'Whosoever will kindle evil will perish by it.'"

[24.1.2] igitur ad hunc Abraham inpugnationem cogitationum nostrarum anxia confessione detulimus, qua ad repetendam prouinciam nostram atque ad reuisendos parentes cotidianis animae aestibus urguebamur. hinc etenim nobis maxima desideriorum nascebatur occasio, quod tanta religione atque pietate parentes nostros praeditos recordabamur, ut eos nequaquam inpedituros nostrum propositum praesumeremus, hoc iugiter mente uoluentes, quod profectum magis ex illorum essemus adsiduitate capturi, nullaque nos corporalium rerum sollicitudine, nullis prospiciendi uictus distentionibus occupandos, illis adfatim omnem cum gaudio praebitionem nostrae necessitatis explentibus.

GETTING AWAY FROM IT ALL

Cassian and Germanus Consult
Abba Abraham of Diolkos

Although it made us uneasy to admit it, we told Abba Abraham about something that had been assailing our thoughts: we had been agitated for days by an urge to return to our homeland and see our families again. Ultimately these desires had arisen because we were reflecting on how deeply religious and dedicated our families are, so much so that we figured they would never be an obstacle to our own plans. We kept thinking about how much more successful we'd be with their help, how deeply engaged we'd be. We wouldn't have to take care of any practicalities at all—we wouldn't even have to think about our next meal—if our families were happily supplying us with everything we possibly needed.

[24.1.3] insuper etiam spe inanium gaudiorum animas pascebamus, credentes nos fructum maximum percepturos de conuersione multorum, qui uelut nostro essent ad uiam salutis exemplo ac monitis dirigendi. tunc praeterea ipsorum locorum situs, in quibus erat maioribus nostris auita possessio, ipsarumque amoenitas iucunda regionum ante oculos pingebatur, quam grate et congrue solitudinis spatiis tenderetur, ita ut non solum delectare monachum possent secreta siluarum, sed etiam maxima uictus praebere conpendia.

[24.1.4] quae omnia praedicto seni cum secundum fidem conscientiae nostrae simpliciter panderemus, nec iam inpugnationum uim tolerare nos posse, nisi nobis per illius medicinam dei gratia subuenisset, profusis lacrimis testaremur, tacitus ille diuque cunctatus atque ad extremum grauiter ingemescens ait.

[24.2.1] Necdum uos desideriis renuntiasse mundanis nec mortificasse concupiscentias pristinas cogitationum uestrarum prodit infirmitas.

We indulged our souls even further with vapid hopes of happiness. We were sure that we would convert many people and reap enormous benefits; they would be guided to the path of salvation by our example and by our words.[46] On top of that, the sheer loveliness of the places where our ancestral estates are located appeared like a work of art before our eyes: how beautifully and charmingly the terrain unfurled into sites of solitude! The retreats in the woodlands there could be attractive to monks—and could also offer an enormous cache of food.

We confided all of this to Abraham frankly, and true to our feelings. Then we wept and said we couldn't handle the intensity of this inner conflict unless, with God's support, he cured us with his medicine. He was quiet for a long time, then at last he groaned loudly and said:

"The weakness of your thoughts has betrayed the fact that you still haven't given up your worldly desires or killed off your old

nam sicut desidiam cordis uestri desideriorum uestrorum peruagatio protestatur, hanc peregrinationem ac parentum absentiam, quam mente potius suscipere debuistis, carne tantummodo sustinetis. sepulta enim haec omnia ac de cordibus uestris euulsa penitus iam fuissent, si uel rationem ipsius abrenuntiationis uel principalem solitudinis causam in qua consistimus cepissetis. [24.2.2] ideoque uos illa otii aegritudine sentio laborare, quae in Prouerbiis ita notatur: in desideriis est omnis otiosus, et iterum: desideria pigrum occidunt.

nam et nobis poterant haec quae commemorastis carnalium commodorum non deesse conpendia, si credidissemus ea nostro conuenire proposito aut talem ex illis amoenitatum uoluptatibus fructum nobis iudicassemus posse conferri, qualis iste est qui de hoc locorum squalore et corporis contritione conquiritur. nec sumus ita parentum solacio destituti, ut nobis desint qui de suis substantiis sustentare nos gaudeant, nisi

tendencies! And these distracting desires testify to the inertia of your heart. You're keeping this pilgrimage and this absence from your families going only in a physical sense—when you should be upholding it in your mind. If you had actually grasped the logic of renunciation and the fundamental reason for our commitment to solitude, all these ideas would have already been put to rest and dug out from the depths of your hearts. For that reason, I think you're afflicted by the laziness that Proverbs describes like this: 'Every lazy person has desires' and 'Desires kill the lazy.'

"It's not like I lack access to the material conveniences you mentioned. I could take advantage of them, too, if I believed that they aligned with my plan, or if I determined that the benefit I derived from those sensuous gratifications would match what I get from this desolation and physical anguish. I'm not bereft of the consolation of my family or cut off from people who would be happy to support me financially,

nobis illa sententia saluatoris occurrens quidquid
ad fotum huius pertinet carnis excluderet, qua
dicitur: qui non reliquerit (siue oderit) patrem
et matrem et filios et fratres, non potest meus
esse discipulus.

[24.2.3] quodsi parentum quoque praesidio
essemus omnimodis desolati, ucl potentum
mundi istius obsequia deesse non possent, qui
promptissima largitate necessitatibus nostris cum
omni gratiarum actione subministrare gauderent.
quorum munificentia sustentati parandi uictus
sollicitudine careremus, nisi nos uehementer
illa prophetica maledictio deterreret. nam male-
dictus, inquit, homo, qui spem suam ponit in
homine, et: nolite confidere in principibus.

potuimus etiam cellulas saltim nostras supra
Nili fluminis alueum conlocantes aquam habere
pro foribus, ne eam a quattuor milibus passuum
nostris cogeremur deferre ceruicibus, nisi nos

either. But I'm confronted with the Savior's saying about distancing ourselves from anything
that pampers us: 'If any man come to me, and
abandon (or hate) not his father, and mother, and
wife, and children, and brethren, he cannot be
my disciple.'

"But even if we were to be totally deprived of
any assistance from our families, the backing of
the powerful people of this world would still
be at our disposal. They would be grateful for
the chance to supply us with what we need, giving liberally without a second thought. We
wouldn't have to bother with stocking up on
food if we were supported by their generosity—
if that prophetic curse didn't forcefully deter us:
'Cursed is the person who has his hope in a
human.' And also: 'Put not your trust in
princes.'[47]

"Or take another case: if we had set up our
dwellings right along the Nile, we could have
gotten water right outside our doors, rather
than having to haul it back on our necks for

ad tolerantiam laboris istius indefessos beatus
apostolus reddens hoc iugiter animaret eloquio,
unusquisque, inquiens, propriam mercedem ac-
cipiet secundum suum laborem.

[24.2.4] nec ignoramus esse nonnulla etiam in
regionibus nostris amoena secreta, in quibus po-
morum copia et hortorum gratia uel ubertas
necessitatem uictus nostri minimo labore corporis expedirent, nisi inpingendam illam nobis
exprobrationem quae ad illum in euangelio di-
recta est diuitem uereremur: quia recepisti con-
solationem tuam in uita tua.

sed despectis illis omnibus et cum uniuersa
mundi huius uoluptate contemptis his tantum
squaloribus delectamur uniuersisque deliciis
horrendam solitudinis istius praeferimus uasti-
tatem neque huic harenarum amaritudini quan-
tasuis uberis glaebae diuitias conparamus, non
temporalia huius corporis lucra, sed aeterna
spiritus emolumenta sectantes.

four miles — except that we were moved by the
words of the blessed apostle to endure this work
over and over again without getting tired: 'Every
man shall receive his own reward according to
his own labor.'

"I'm not unaware that there are lovely retreats
in our environs, too, where the fruit is bounti-
ful and the gardens generous, and the abun-
dance of food would meet our needs with
barely any effort on our part — except we take
seriously that compelling assertion made to the
rich man in the Gospel: 'Remember that thou
in thy lifetime receivedst thy good things.'

"But when we've rejected all that, when we've
devalued it along with the rest of the world's at-
tractions, when we're seduced only by the desert, when we prefer the intimidating wilderness
of this isolation of ours to all the world's charms,
and when we think that no fertile soil, however
rich it is, can rival this bitter sandscape: *then* we
are in pursuit of everlasting gains for the spirit,
rather than fleeting benefits to the body.

[24.2.5] parum est enim renuntiasse monachum semel, id est in primordio conuersionis
suae contempsisse praesentia, nisi eis cotidie re-
nuntiare perstiterit. usque ad finem namque
huius uitae illud nobis dicendum est cum
propheta: et diem hominis non desideraui, tu
scis. unde et dominus in euangelio si quis, inquit, uult post me uenire, abnegct semet ipsum
et tollat crucem suam cotidie et sequatur me.

[24.3.1] Et idcirco ei, qui de interioris hominis puritate peruigilem sollicitudinem gerit, ex-
petenda sunt loca, quae mentem eius nulla ad
culturae distentionem ubertatis suae fecunditate
sollicitent nec de cellulae fixa atque inmobili sta-
tione proturbent atque ad aliquod subdiuale
opus prodire conpellant, et ita uelut in apertum
effusis cogitationibus omnem mentis directionem ac subtilissimum certe illius destinationis
intuitum per diuersa dispergat.
[24.3.2] quae a nemine prorsus quamuis sol-
licito ac uigilanti uel caueri poterunt uel uideri,

"It's really not enough for monks to perform the act of renunciation just once, to discard what they've got when they first convert to monasticism. They have to keep renouncing it every day, until the end of this life. What the prophet said applies to us: 'I have not desired the day of man, thou knowest.' And this is what the Lord is saying in the Gospel: 'If any man will come after me, let him deny himself, and take up his cross daily, and follow me.'

"And so a monk who is always keeping an eye on his inner clarity should seek out locations that won't distract him with thoughts about farming them for high yields, and which won't drive him from the designated fixed spot of his cell and force him do some other work out in the open. Once outside, his thoughts will basically spread out everywhere. Every line of thinking, even his crystal-clear view of his short-term goal, will be scattered in all directions.

"Nobody, no matter how careful and alert they are, can avoid these risks or even perceive

nisi qui corpus atque animum suum iugiter intra parietum saepta concluserit, ut ita quis uelut piscator egregius uictum sibi apostolica arte prospiciens in tranquillissimo cordis sui profundo agmina cogitationum natantia intentus atque inmobilis captet et tamquam de prominenti scopulo curiose profunda prospectans, quas ad se hamo adtrahere debeat salutari, quas uero tamquam malos et noxios pisces neglegat ac refutet, sagaci discretione diiudicet. [24.4.1] In hac ergo unusquisque custodia iugiter perseuerans efficaciter illud inplebit, quod per Abbacuc prophetam satis euidenter exprimitur: super custodiam meam stabo et ascendam super petram, et speculabor ut uideam quid loquatur in me, et quid respondeam ad arguentem me.

quod quanti laboris ac difficultatis sit, experimentis illorum, qui in illa Calami seu Porphyrionis heremo commorantur, manifestissime

them unless they keep their body and mind walled in at all times. They should work like an expert fisherman with apostolic know-how, focusing on the shoals of thoughts swimming in the quiet deep of their heart, casting their gaze on their next meal, lying in wait without moving a muscle, peering into the depths like they're perched on an overhanging ledge. And using their shrewd discernment they should differentiate which thoughts to hook and pull in, and which to disregard and release like bad and poisonous fish. Anyone who keeps watch like this nonstop will successfully fulfill what the prophet Habakkuk was so obviously describing: 'I will stand at my watch post and station myself on a rock. And I will keep watch to see what he will say to me, and what I should answer to my reproof.'

"The experiences of the monks who dwelled in the desert of Calamus or Porphyry demonstrate very clearly how much work this is, and how hard it is, too.[48] These monks are much

conprobatur. [24.4.2] nam cum longiore solitudinis interuallo ab uniuersis urbibus et habitaculis
hominum quam heremus Sciti diuidantur (septem
siquidem uel octo mansionibus uastissimae solitudinis deserta penetrantes uix ad cellarum suarum
secreta perueniunt), tamen, quia illic agriculturae
dediti claustris minime cohibentur, cum ad haec
squalida in quibus degimus uel illa Scitiotica
uenerint loca, tantis cogitationum aestibus, tanta
animi anxietate uexantur, ut quasi rudes et qui
solitudinis exercitia ne leuiter quidem aliquando
contigerint commorationem cellae et quietis silen-
tia tolerare non possint atque ex eis statim excussi
tamquam expertes ac nouicii proturbentur.

[24.4.3] non enim sedare interioris hominis
motus et cogitationum suarum tempestatibus
obuiare iugi sollicitudine ac perseueranti intentione didicerunt, qui subdiualibus cotidie operibus desudantes tota die sub aëria inanitate non
solum carne, uerum etiam mente peruolitant et

more isolated from cities and populations than the desert of Scetis is: after traveling the vast expanses of uninhabited desert for seven or eight days you would only just reach their remote dwellings. But they're not really restricted to their cells because they do farmwork there. So when they visit the crude sites where I live, or the ones at Scetis, they're agitated by so many thoughts and by such mental distress that—like novices or monks who haven't trained in isolation, not even a little bit—they can't bear to stay in their cell and keep still, so they give up in no time at all. They're rattled like inexperienced beginners.

"That's because they haven't learned how to quell the movements of their inner person, or how to confront their stormy thoughts with nonstop concern and steadfast attentiveness. While they're sweating away at work outside under the great big sky, all day every day, it's not just their bodies that are bustling around. Their minds are, too, and with every step they

cogitationes suas cum mobilitate corporea passim in aperta diffundunt. et idcirco nec multiuolam animi sui sentiunt uanitatem nec eius lubricos possunt cohercere discursus, et contritionem spiritus non ferentes intolerabilem sibi ipsam silentii sui aestimant iugitatem, ac laboriosis ruris operibus indefessi uincuntur otio et quietis suae diuturnitate lassantur.

[24.5.1] Nec mirum si in cella quis residens, quasi in artissimum claustrum cogitationibus congregatis, anxietatum multitudine suffocetur, quae de carceribus habitaculi cum homine prorumpentes continuo uelut equi effrenes per diuersa peruolitant. sed cum ad praesens de suis uelut stabulis euagentur, capitur statim aliquod uel breue ac triste solacium: cum uero corpore ad cellam propriam remeante rursum quasi ad sedem suam cuncta cogitationum caterua recucurrerit, grauiores excitat stimulos ipsa inueteratae licentiae consuetudo.

take they pour their thoughts out into the open. So they don't notice the mind's aimless cravings, and they can't keep its slippery meanderings in check. Because they can't bear spiritual anguish, they find endless silence to be unbearable. And after so much tough agrarian work, they succumb to inactivity, then the lengthiness of their down time wears them out!

"It's no wonder that a monk staying in his cell, stuffed into confinement with his thoughts, would be choked by all sorts of anxieties—and that when the monk leaves his dwelling, these thoughts would immediately break out from their prison, galloping all over the place like unbridled horses. When they wander out of their 'stables,' the monk immediately feels some relief. But that moment is fleeting and sad, because when the whole herd of thoughts comes running back to his cell along with his body, as if they're heading home, his old habitual lack of restraint riles them up again even more severely.

[24.5.2] hi ergo qui necdum possunt uel no-
runt uoluntatum suarum instigationibus reluc-
tari, cum acedia pectus insolitum uehementius
inpugnante intra cellam fuerint anxiati, si pro-
grediendi saepius libertatem sibi remissa districtionis lege concesserint, acriorem aduersum se
pestem hoc ut putant remedio suscitabunt: sicut
gelidissimae aquae haustu uim internarum
febrium quidam rcstinguere posse se credunt,
cum utique ex hoc accendi ignem illum constet
potius quam sedari, siquidem momentaneam
illam releuationem multo grauior consequatur
adflictio.

[24.6.1] Quamobrem ita monachi omnis intentio in unum semper est defigenda cuncta-
rumque cogitationum eius ortus atque circuitus
in id ipsum, id est ad memoriam dei strenue
reuocandi,
    uelut si quis teretis absidae cameram uolens
in sublime concludere subtilissimi illius centri
lineam iugiter circumducat ac secundum illius

"So when monks can't or won't resist the prodding of their own wills, and they're tormented in their cell by a restless dissatisfaction that catches them off guard and attacks them really violently: if their reaction is to abandon the principle of restrictiveness and give themselves free rein to go out, this supposed 'cure' will only intensify the corrosive disease that afflicts them. It's like how some people believe that they can chill the heat of internal fevers by drinking ice-cold water, when of course this will obviously fuel the fire rather than put it out, since that momentary alleviation is followed by pain that is much more severe.

"For that reason a monk's complete attention should always be fixed on one thing, and all his rising and revolving thoughts should be drawn back quickly to it alone—to the memory of God.

"It's like when someone wants to construct a domed vault: they encircle the axis over and over with extreme precision, and adhering to this

certissimam normam omnem rutunditatis parilitatem structurae colligat disciplina. [24.6.2] qui uero
eam absque illius medietatis examine consum-
mare quamuis summa artis aut ingenii praesump-
tione temptauerit, inpossibile est ut aequalitatem
circuitus illius sine errore custodiat aut quantum
uerae rutunditatis pulchritudini errando sub-
traxerit solo deprehendat aspectu, nisi ad illum
indicem ueritatis sempcr recurrens atque eius
arbitrio interiorem operis sui ambitum exteri-
oremque castigans tam excelsae magnitudinis
molem unius puncti lege concludat.

[24.6.3] ita etiam mens nostra, nisi solam domini caritatem uelut centrum inmobiliter fixum
per uniuersa operum molitionumque nostrarum
momenta circumagens probabili ut ita dixerim
circino caritatis omnium cogitationum uel ap-
tauerit uel reppulerit qualitatem, nequaquam
structuram illam aedificii spiritalis, cuius Paulus

exact measurement enables them to produce a perfectly round structure.[49] People who try to accomplish this without taking that center into account, no matter how confident they are in their skill or talent, will find that it's truly impossible to maintain a perfect circle without any mistakes by relying on sight alone to catch any deviations from perfect roundness. They can enclose such a colossal towering structure only with recourse to a single point. They have to keep referring back to that true focus while making calculated adjustments to the inner and outer circumferences of the dome as they go.[50]

"Our mind also works that way. In every moment of our construction and demolition projects, it should revolve exclusively around the love of God as its fixed unchanging center. Using this reliable compass of love (as I might describe it), it should accommodate or curtail its thoughts, depending on the property of each one. Otherwise the mind will lack the real skills to construct that spiritual building of which

est architectus, probabili arte molietur, nec pul-
chritudinem domus illius possidebit, quam
beatus Dauid in corde suo domino cupiens exhibere domine, inquit, dilexi decorem domus
tuae, et locum habitationis gloriae tuae, sed in-
decoram in corde suo atque indignam spiritui
sancto domum continuoque lapsuram inpru-
denter adtollet, non glorificandus beati cohabi-
tatoris hospitio, sed ruina constructionis suae
lugubriter opprimendus.

[24.18] GERMANVS: Inter cetera inlusionum
errorumque nostrorum genera, quae nos ad desiderium patriae nostrae, sicut beatitudo tua
sollerti mentis perspexit intuitu, uana spiritalium commodorum pollicitatione flammauerant,
etiam haec uel maxima extitit causa, quod interdum a fratribus frequentati iugi secreto ac
diuturno silentio secundum desiderium nostrum

Paul is the architect, and it won't attain the beauty of the house that the blessed David wanted to offer in his heart to the Lord: 'Lord,' he said, 'I have loved the habitation of thy house, and the place where thine honor dwelleth.' Instead it will inadvertently produce an ugly house in its heart that isn't fit for the Holy Spirit and is liable to give way at any time. It won't be a hospitable place for the Blessed Guest! Instead of celebrating, the mind will collapse in sadness along with its shoddy construction."

LATER IN THE CONVERSATION WITH ABRAHAM

Germanus said: "Your blessedness, you have perceptively seen right through our misguided fantasies, which had been fueling our desire for our birthplace with the empty assurance that things would be spiritually convenient there. But this one major issue still stands out: in our current circumstances, our fellow monks keep paying us visits, and there's no way that we can

nequaquam possumus inhaerere. per quod necesse est cursum atque mensuram cotidianae
continentiae nostrae, quam pro castigatione corporis indisruptam perpetuo cupimus retentare,
nonnullis fratribus superuenientibus intercidi.
quod sine dubio nullatenus in nostra prouincia
credimus euenturum, in qua aut nullum aut certe
rarissimum professionis huius uirum inuenire
possibile est.

[24.19.1] ABRAHAM: Inrationabilis atque
inconsideratae districtionis, immo potius summi
teporis indicium est nequaquam ab hominibus
frequentari. qui enim in hac quam arripuit uia
nimium tardis passibus graditur ac secundum
anteriorem hominem conuersatur, aequum est
ut ad eum non dicam sanctorum, sed ne hominum quidem ullus adueniat. uos autem, si uera
atque perfecta domini nostri dilectione flagratis
et deum, qui utique caritas est, pleno spiritus feruore sectamini, ad quaelibet loca inaccessibilia
fugeritis, necesse est ea ab hominibus frequentari, quantoque uos propiores deo amoris diuini

stick to the seclusion and enduring silence we long for. When our various brothers show up, we have to cut our daily routine of self-restraint short, even though for the sake of physical discipline we want to keep it up forever without any breaks. We're certain this wouldn't happen at home. Where we're from, you would never—or at least only very rarely—come across another monk!"

Abraham said: "Never being visited by other people is an unreasonably strict policy, and a thoughtless one, too. Worse, it's a sign of total lukewarmness. A person who walks really sluggishly down the road he's taken and reverts into the kind of person he was before he left: it's fair to say that not a single holy person—or even single regular person—would join up with him. But if you burn with a true and perfect love for our Lord, and follow God (who is love itself) with your spirit on full boil, and flee to some remote place? Then other people will inevitably visit! Because the more that the heat of divine

ardor effecerit, tanto ad uos maior sanctorum fratrum confluet multitudo. [24.19.2] non enim potest secundum sententiam domini ciuitas abscondi super montem posita, quia diligentes, inquit, me, dominus, glorificabo, qui autem me contemnunt, erunt ignobiles.

uerumtamen nosse debetis hanc esse subtilissimam diaboli calliditatem, hanc occultissimam foueam, in quam miscrabiles et incautos quosque praecipitat, ut, dum eis maiora promittit, necessaria cotidiani fructus emolumenta subripiat, abstrusiores scilicet ac uastiores solitudines expeti debere persuadens easque uelut miris amoenitatibus consitas in eorum corde depingens. ignota etiam quaedam et quae penitus nusquam sunt loca uelut cognita ac praeparata nostraeque potestati iam dedita et absque ulla difficultate possidenda confingit. [24.19.3] homines quoque regionis illius tractabiles et ad uiam salutis sequaces esse mentitur,

love brings you closer to God, the more an increasingly large number of holy monks will flock to you. According to what the Lord said, a city set on a hill can't be hidden. 'For I will honor those who love me,' he said, 'and those who despise me shall be treated with contempt.'

"In any case, you should recognize the devil's savvy cunning for what it is. It's a hidden pitfall that wretched and reckless people fall into: while he's promising them better things, he's stealing the supplies they worked hard to get. More specifically, he's making the case that they should seek out more distant and desolate wildernesses, and he's painting a picture of those places in their hearts as if they're marvelously idyllic. He even fabricates locations that they've never heard of, which don't actually exist, as places that seem familiar and ready and waiting for us to take over and move in without a hitch. He also falsely promises that the inhabitants of these hypothetical places can be easily persuaded and led to the path of salvation.

ut, dum illic uberiores fructus animae pollice-
tur, praesentia lucra fraudulenter eripiat. nam cum
unusquisque hac uana spe a seniorum contuber-
nio separatus atque omnibus quae frustra sibimet
in suo corde depinxerat fuerit destitutus, uelut
de profundissimo sopore consurgens nihil ex his
quae somniauerat expergefactus inueniet.

[24.19.4] itaque eum diabolus maioribus uitae
huius necessitatibus et inextricabilibus laqueis
inretitum ne respirare quidem ad haec quae sibi
ipse promiserat aliquando permittet, eumque non
iam illis quas ante uitauerat raris ac spiritalibus
fratrum uisitationibus, sed cotidianis saecularium incursionibus obligatum ne ad mediocrem
quidem anachoreseos quietem ac disciplinam
umquam redire patietur.

"So as he dangles the prospect of more fruitful benefits to the soul off over there, he's using sleight of hand to snatch the gains they've already got. And once they're severed from the companionship of their elders by this empty hope, and deprived of everything that they'd misguidedly imagined for themselves, they will feel like they've risen from a deep sleep only to find no sign, once they're awake, of anything they'd dreamed about.

"Eventually, once a monk has become entangled in the labyrinthine traps and overwhelming forces of this life, the devil doesn't even give him a moment to catch his breath and think fondly about what he'd been promised. And he doesn't ever let him go back to those precious spiritual visits from his brothers that he'd avoided in the past—or even to the discipline and ordinary quiet of a hermit's life. Instead the monk remains tied up, day after day, in the intrusions of laypeople.

[24.20.1] Illa quoque remissionis et humanitatis intercapedo gratissima, quae nonnumquam pro aduentu fratrum interuenire consueuit, licet molesta uobis ac fugienda uideatur,

tamen quam sit utilis et salubris tam corpori quam spiritui nostro, paucis patienter adtendite. [24.20.2] saepe accidit non dicam nouiciis et infirmis, sed etiam experientissimis atque perfectis, ut, nisi mentis eorum directio et censura quibusdam mollita fuerit uicissitudinum laxamentis, aut in teporem spiritus aut certe in perniciosam corporis ualitudinem conlabatur. et idcirco a prudentibus atque perfectis, cum intercesserit fratrum etiam crebra uisitatio, non solum toleranda patienter, sed etiam gratanter est amplectenda:

[24.20.3] primum quod prouocat nos auidius semper solitudinis desiderare secreta (nam quodammodo cursum nostrum dum creditur reti-

"Sure, sometimes your fellow monks will interrupt you by showing up here, but although it might seem like an annoyance you should avoid, such a relaxing and humanizing break is something to be deeply thankful for.

"Bear with me for a minute and think about how beneficial and healthful this is for our body as well as our spirit. If our intense concentration isn't alleviated by some kind of pleasant change of pace, the mind will slip either into spiritual lukewarmness or at least into some life-threatening physical illness. I would say that this often happens to new monks or weak monks and even to very experienced and perfect monks. For this reason, thoughtful and expert monks should do more than just tolerate the interruptions of their brothers' frequent visits. They should welcome them with gratitude, for two reasons.

"First: such visits keep up our cravings for solitary retreats. (It might seem like our visitors are holding us back, but actually they enable us

nere, infatigabilem iugemque conseruat: qui si
nullo interdum obice tardaretur, usque ad finem
contendere indefessa pernicitate non posset),

deinde quod necessitatem reficiendi corpus-
culi cum fructu humanitatis indulget, maiora
nobis conferens lucra cum iucundissimo corporis laxamento quam illa sunt quae per abstinen-
tiae fatigationem fuerant adquirenda. super qua
re aptissimam conparationem antiqua narratione
uulgatam breuiter indicabo.

[24.21.1] Fertur beatissimus Iohannes, cum
perdicem suis manibus molliter demulceret, phi-
losophum quendam ritu ad se uenatorio ueni-
entem subito conspexisse. qui miratus quod uir
tantae opinionis ac famae ad tam parua et humilia se oblectamenta submitteret, tune es, inquit,
ille Iohannes, cuius fama insignis atque celeber-
rima me quoque summo desiderio tuae agnitionis

to keep going without getting tired. A person who *isn't* slowed down by any impediments along the way can't make it to the end with the same agility he started with.)

"Second: they accommodate our measly body's need to be restored with human company. A really nice break for our body is much more advantageous than what we could have gained by wearing ourselves out in withholding it completely. Speaking of which, I'll briefly mention an analogous case from an old story everyone knows.

"It is said that the most blessed monk John was once gently petting a partridge, when suddenly he spotted a philosopher of one persuasion or another coming toward him in full hunting gear. The philosopher was amazed that a man who was so well known and highly regarded was stooping to such a childish and low-class form of amusement.[51] He said, 'Aren't you the John who is so eminent and famous that even I was lured by an overwhelming desire to get to

inlexit? cur ergo oblectamentis tam uilioribus occuparis?

[24.21.2] cui beatus Iohannes: quid est, inquit, quod manu tua gestas?

at ille: arcus, inquit.

et cur, ait, non eum tensum semper ubique circumfers?

cui ille respondit: non oportet, ne iugi curuamine rigoris fortitudo laxata mollescat atque depereat, et cum oportuerit ut fortiora in aliquam feram spicula dirigantur, rigore iam per nimietatem continuae intentionis amisso uiolentior ictus non possit emitti.

[24.21.3] nec nostri, inquit beatus Iohannes, animi te offendat, o iuuenis, tam parua haec breuisque laxatio, quae nisi remissione quadam rigorem intentionis suae interdum releuet ac relaxet, inremisso uigore lentescens uirtuti spiritus, cum necessitas poscit, obsecundare non poterit.

know you? Why are you busying yourself with such worthless amusements?'

"The blessed John replied, 'What are you holding in your hand?'

'A bow,' the philosopher said.

'Okay, and why don't you walk around everywhere with it drawn all the time?'

'That's not how it works,' the philosopher said. 'If the bow were always bent, the stiff strength it has when it's relaxed would get too elastic and give out. And when it came time to aim a flurry of arrows at a wild animal, the loss of stiffness caused by excessive and constant tension would make it impossible to shoot for high impact.'

'Well then, kiddo,' said the blessed John, 'don't take issue with my mind's relaxation, as small and brief as it is. It takes some sort of release every now and then to lighten and loosen the tautness of the mind's attention. When duty calls, the spirit won't be able to step up if relentless force has made its strength go slack.'"

[24.26.18] Tali beatus Abraham de inlusionis nostrae uel origine uel medella disputatione disseruit atque oculis quodammodo nostris cogitationum quas diabolus auctor ingesserat propalauit insidias nosque ad desiderium uerae mortificationis accendit, quo etiam multos, licet incompto haec omnia sermone digesta sint, credimus inflammandos. nam licet summorum patrum flagrantissimos sensus tepida eloquii nostri fauilla contexerit, plurimorum tamen algorem, qui remotis uerborum cineribus uiuacitatem latentium sensuum suscitare uoluerint, calefaciendum putamus.

[24.26.19] sed ad uos, o sancti fratres, non utique hunc ignem, quem dominus uenit mittere in terram et quem nimium ardere desiderat, ita spiritu praesumptionis elatus emisi, ut quasi feruentissimum propositum uestrum caloris

THE END OF THE CONVERSATION WITH ABRAHAM (AND THE ENTIRE *COLLATIONES*)

And that was how the blessed Abraham addressed the cause and the cure of our delusion. In a way, he opened our eyes to the traps that the diabolic culprit had set for our thoughts. He fired us up with a desire to truly kill all that off. And we believe that many others, once they've processed all of this, will be ignited by it, too, even though the writing isn't polished. The embers of our eloquence convey the blazing insights of the peerless elders with only a faint heat, but we still think that they'll warm the chill felt by many people—who may want to use the stray cinders of our words to stoke hidden insights to life.

As for you, oh holy brothers: the Lord came to send this fire on the earth, and he longs for it to burn boundlessly. I'm not so spiritually conceited as to presume that in feeding that fire I'll add any heat to your own ragingly hot resolve.

huius adiectione succenderem, sed ut uobis maior apud filios esset auctoritas, si id, quod ipsi non mortuo uerborum sono, sed uiuo docetis exemplo, etiam summorum atque antiquissimorum patrum praecepta confirment.

superest ut me periculosissima hactenus tempestate iactatum nunc ad tutissimum silentii portum spiritalis orationum uestrarum aura comitetur.

No. I do it so that you'll influence the next generation more powerfully if you teach not by the dead sound of words but by your own living example, backed up by the advice of the best and most ancient elders.

Until now I've been tossed all around in a treacherous storm. Now it's up to the spiritual breeze of your prayers to sweep me to the safe harbor of silence.

NOTES

1. For the historical context: Jamie Kreiner, *The Wandering Mind: What Medieval Monks Tell Us about Distraction* (New York: Liveright, 2023).
2. Inbar Graiver, *Asceticism of the Mind: Forms of Attention and Self-Transformation in Late Antique Monasticism* (Toronto: Pontifical Institute of Mediaeval Studies, 2018); Jessica L. Wright, *The Care of the Brain in Early Christianity* (Oakland: University of California Press, 2022).
3. David Brakke, *Demons and the Making of the Monk: Spiritual Combat in Early Christianity* (Cambridge, MA: Harvard University Press, 2006).
4. Columba Stewart, *Cassian the Monk* (New York: Oxford University Press, 1998), 107; likewise Philip Rousseau, "Cassian, Contemplation and the Coenobitic Life," *Journal of Ecclesiastical History* 26 (1975): 113–26.
5. For Cassian and his social contexts: Stewart, *Cassian the Monk*; Richard J. Goodrich,

Contextualizing Cassian: Aristocrats, Asceticism, and Reformation in Fifth-Century Gaul (Oxford: Oxford University Press, 2007).

6. *Sayings of the Desert Fathers* [=*AP/G*], trans. Benedicta Ward, rev. ed. (Kalamazoo, MI: Cistercian Publications, 1984), 112–15. In addition to the Alphabetical Collection cited here, Cassian also appears in various versions of the Systematic Collection: see the *Monastica* database at https://monastica.ht.lu.se/.

7. Ferrandus, *Vita Fulgentii* 8, trans. Robert B. Eno, as "Life of the Blessed Bishop Fulgentius," in *Fulgentius: Selected Works* (Washington, DC: Catholic University of America Press, 1997); Jonas of Bobbio, *Vita Iohannis* 18, trans. Alexander O'Hara and Ian Wood, as "Life of John of Réomé," in *Jonas of Bobbio: Life of Columbanus, Life of John of Réomé, and Life of Vedast* (Liverpool: Liverpool University Press, 2017), nodding to *Collationes* 9.2.3–9.3.2; *Regula Benedicti* 42.3–5, 73.5, ed. Timothy Fry et al., as *RB 1980: The Rule of St. Benedict in Latin and English with Notes* (Collegeville, MN: Liturgical, 1981). On the uncertain origins of the *RB* and its mixed early reception: Albrecht Diem, Diem, *The*

Pursuit of Salvation: Community, Space, and Discipline in Early Medieval Monasticism, with a Critical Edition and Translation of the "Regula cuiusdam ad uirgines" (Turnhout: Brepols, 2021), 331–45.

8. Cassian's ethics: see esp. Niki Kasumi Clements, *Sites of the Ascetic Self: John Cassian and Christian Ethical Formation* (Notre Dame: University of Notre Dame Press, 2020); Stewart, *Cassian the Monk*. Cassian's influence: see, e.g., Conrad Leyser, *Authority and Asceticism from Augustine to Gregory the Great* (Oxford: Clarendon, 2000), esp. 33–61; Albrecht Diem, *Das monastische Experiment: Die Rolle der Keuschheit bei der Entstehung des westlichen Klosterwesens* (Münster: LIT, 2004), 95–114; Albrecht Diem, *Pursuit of Salvation*, esp. 538–54. Diversity of monastic culture: see, e.g., *The Cambridge History of Medieval Monasticism in the Latin West*, vol. 1, *Origins to the Eleventh Century*, ed. Alison I. Beach and Isabelle Cochelin (Cambridge: Cambridge University Press, 2020).

9. Cassian wrote the *Collationes* in three phases, as he notes in his introductions to each installment: originally he'd intended to stop after book 10, but

he went on to expand the text twice (with books 11–17 and books 18–24).

10. Mihaly Csikszentmihalyi, *Beyond Boredom and Anxiety: The Experience of Play in Work and Games* (San Francisco: Jossey-Bass, 1975), with contributions by Isabella Csikszentmihalyi.

11. The standard Latin edition is *Johannis Cassiani Opera Pars II: Conlationes XXIIII*, ed. Michael Petschenig, Corpus Scriptorum Ecclesiasticorum Latinorum 13 (Vienna: Österreichische Akademie der Wissenschaften, 1886). For a complete English translation, see *The Conferences*, trans. Boniface Ramsey, Ancient Christian Writers 57 (New York: Newman Press, 1997).

12. Eugippius, *Regula* 30–31 [=*Collationes* 12.2.1–3, 12.7.2–4, with some cuts], ed. Fernando Villegas and Adalbert de Vogüé, Corpus Scriptorum Ecclesiasticorum Latinorum 87 (Vienna: Hölder-Pichler-Tempsky, 1976). MSS of Cassian: see Petschenig's discussion of the manuscript tradition in *Johannis Cassiani Opera Pars I*, Corpus Scriptorum Ecclesiasticorum Latinorum 17 (Vienna: Österreichische Akademie der Wissenschaften, 1888), xxx–lxxi, xcv–ciiii.

13. This is one reason I don't distinguish biblical quotations in the text: many readers tend to skip over them when they're demarcated by italics or footnotes. The other reason is that monks themselves had internalized some books of the Bible so deeply that they often slipped seamlessly between its words and theirs. Readers who are interested in these intertextualities can consult the notes in Ramsey's translation of the *Conferences*.

14. This position is something of a compromise between those of Mark Polizzotti, *Sympathy for the Traitor: A Translation Manifesto* (Cambridge, MA: MIT Press, 2018); Edith Grossman, *Why Translation Matters* (New Haven, CT: Yale University Press, 2010); and Lawrence Venuti, *The Translator's Invisibility: A History of Translation*, 2nd ed. (London: Routledge, 2008).

15. See 1.5.3 and 9.12.1. I've used three translations of the Bible here—the King James, the Douay-Rheims, and *A New English Translation of the Septuagint*, ed. Albert Pietersma and Benjamin G. Wright, corr. ed. (Oxford: Oxford University Press, 2014)—occasionally with small modifications. The choice depended on Cassian's

Latin, since monks themselves used different versions and translations and were often working from memory.

16. *Collationes* 16.1 (not included in this translation).

17. For the Stoics, *passio* most basically meant "emotion" in a negative sense—any emotional investment, impulse, or reaction that was tied to inappropriate ideas about what was good and bad. Brad Inwood, *Ethics and Human Action in Early Stoicism* (Oxford: Clarendon, 1985), 127–81; Richard Sorabji, *Emotion and Peace of Mind: From Stoic Agitation to Christian Temptation* (Oxford: Oxford University Press, 2000). Cassian drew on the Stoic interest in surmounting such emotions to attain a state of tranquility and freedom from disturbance, but he also valued certain states of mind that we would classify today as emotional (see, e.g., 9.26), so I've opted for a mix of translations that point toward the technical meaning of *passio*.

18. Luke Dysinger, *Psalmody and Prayer in the Writings of Evagrius Ponticus* (Oxford: Oxford University Press, 2005), 76–81; Augustine Michael Casiday, "*Apatheia* and Sexuality in the Thought of Augustine and Cassian," *St. Vladimir's*

Theological Quarterly 45, no. 4 (2001): 359–94; Stewart, *Cassian the Monk*, 42–47.

19. In 9.26–9.30, Cassian and Germanus will speak with Abba Isaac about the role of weeping in monastic practice.

20. I've often opted for gender-neutral language when Cassian uses the singular masculine—partly because Cassian founded a women's monastery in addition to one for men, and partly because monks in Gaul in subsequent centuries tended to treat their handbooks and guidelines as "unisex" documents: Albrecht Diem, "The Gender of the Religious: Wo/Men and the Invention of Monasticism," in *The Oxford Handbook of Women and Gender in Medieval Europe*, ed. Judith Bennett and Ruth Karras (Oxford: Oxford University Press, 2013), 432–46, esp. 437–40.

21. See "Notes on the Translation."

22. Here Cassian (and Moses) are paraphrasing Phil. 3:14 by swapping out the verse's use of *skopos/destinatum* for *finis*. They are taking Paul to mean that the "prize of the high calling" is actually the ultimate goal (*finis*)—given that, as they already pointed out, Paul says in Rom. 6:22 that

everlasting life is the *finis*—whereas the immediate goal (*skopos*) is in fact the navigational device that will help him reach the end. This was monastic biblical interpretation in action: through a pairing of two passages from Paul's letters, whose keywords are linked to their current discussion, Cassian/Moses build out their conceptual schematic of immediate and long-term goals.

23. These are all instruments for making documents and books—everyday tools for many monks: Roger Bagnall, "The Educational and Cultural Background of Egyptian Monks," in *Monastic Education in Late Antiquity: The Transformation of Classical Paideia*, ed. Lillian I. Larsen and Samuel Rubenson (Cambridge: Cambridge University Press, 2018), 75–100; Chrysi Kotsifou, "Books and Book Production in the Monastic Communities of Byzantine Egypt," in *The Early Christian Book*, ed. William Klingshirn and Linda Safran (Washington, DC: Catholic University of America Press, 2007), 48–66.

24. See "Notes on the Translation."

25. Cassian and other monks who took a cue from Evagrius sometimes spoke of thoughts as separate from themselves, and they worked to detect

and screen them in order to prevent the unwanted ones from influencing them: see, e.g., 24.3.2, and Inbar Graiver, "'I Think' vs. 'The Thought Tells Me': What Grammar Teaches Us about the Monastic Self," *Journal of Early Christian Studies* 25 (2017): 255–79.

26. *Lolium* is a hardy grass that mimics cultivated cereals and grows among them but is toxic to humans. It was a notorious plant in Latin literature. And because some ancient naturalists supposed that weeds were generated by faulty seeds—that is, seeds with *vitia*—it was all the better as a metaphor for Cassian: Paolo Squatriti, *Weeds and the Carolingians: Empire, Culture, and Nature in Frankish Europe, AD 750–900* (Cambridge: Cambridge University Press, 2022), 114–23.

27. For Cassian, the inner person or *homo interior* amounted to one's thoughts, feelings, and ethical orientation—all of which were interdependent with one's behaviors and actions: Rousseau, "Cassian, Contemplation and the Coenobitic Life."

28. Weeping was one sign that a monk was emotionally invested in his or her goals and therefore primed to concentrate on the divine: see 9.26.

29. Later in their consultations, Cassian and Germanus will get more advice from Abba Isaac and Abba Nesteros about the value of the workings of the memory (*Coll.* 10.8–14, 14.10–13).

30. Isaac/Cassian may have been thinking of a ridgepole rather than a king post: see Roger B. Ulrich, *Roman Woodworking* (New Haven, CT: Yale University Press, 2007), 296. Either way, the metaphor is a bit loose with the principles of structural engineering, and Cassian will go on to use *culmen* in the more general sense of "summit" (9.7.4, 10.8.4), synonymous with *excelsa* (10.8.2).

31. *Simplicitas* and *humilitas*: Cassian is playing on these nouns to encapsulate both a foundation's physical features (straightforwardly built and low lying), and a monk's ideal traits (honest and unassuming).

32. *Puras manus*: rendered as "holy" hands in King James but literally meaning "clean" or "pure" hands, tied to Cassian's concept of the clear heart by virtue of the shared root (*puritas cordis*).

33. "Not" is Isaac/Cassian's insertion into the Septuagint's version of Joel 1:5: "Sober up,

drunkards, from their wine." This gloss accentuates the parallel with Isaiah 29:9 in the next section.

34. Early Christian monks often pictured demons as black figures or more specifically as Ethiopians, even though some of their colleagues—including the famous Abba Moses of book 1—were themselves Black Ethiopians. The demonic imagery turned on Mediterranean and Christian associations of Black bodies with otherness, evil, sexuality, and power. But blackness was also an attribute with which all monks identified. They knew that external appearances weren't sure guides to spiritual truths and that every person was simultaneously fallible and redeemable: black could be white, white could be black, everyone was both black and white. Brakke, *Demons and the Making of the Monk*, 157–81; Cord J. Whitaker, *Black Metaphors: How Modern Racism Emerged from Medieval Race-Thinking* (Philadelphia: University of Pennsylvania Press, 2019).

35. For *excessus* as divinely catalyzed ecstasy or transport (versus other kinds of *excessus*), see A.M.C. Casiday, *Tradition and Theology in St. John*

Cassian (Oxford: Oxford University Press, 2007), 203–14; Stewart, *Cassian the Monk*, 116–22.

36. Literally, "fatty" or "rich": the connotations here are positive.

37. On the capacious meaning of *compunctio* in this section see Stewart, *Cassian the Monk*, 122–28.

38. For Cassian and for many other Christians in late antiquity and the early Middle Ages, weeping was a sign of genuine attention and investment: a person who wept was fully registering the ethical dimensions of, and divine involvement in, the situation at hand: see further Jamie Kreiner, "A Generic Mediterranean: Hagiography in the Early Middle Ages," in *East and West in the Early Middle Ages: The Merovingian Kingdoms in Mediterranean Perspective*, ed. Stefan Esders et al. (Cambridge: Cambridge University Press, 2019), 202–17, at 209–10.

39. Isaac/Cassian are referring to Psalm 101 in the numbering of the Septuagint and Vulgate, equivalent to Psalm 102 in most modern versions, which follow the numbering of the Hebrew Bible.

40. *Materia* and *formula* were technical terms in ancient classrooms; I've rendered them in various

ways to capture their pedagogical functions. See Mary Carruthers, *The Craft of Thought: Meditation, Rhetoric, and the Making of Images, 400–1200* (Cambridge: Cambridge University Press, 1998), 74–76; Philip Rousseau, *Ascetics, Authority, and the Church in the Age of Jerome and Cassian* (Oxford: Oxford University Press, 1978), 223–27.

41. Cassian/Germanus are caricaturing a particular subset of *meditatio*, an analytical and associative mode of thinking that monks used to link different scriptural passages and other texts together to come to a wider understanding about some topic. Critics of this form of meditation thought that it encouraged the mind to wander; proponents saw it as a technique for harnessing the mind's free-ranging tendencies in the service of critical thinking. Cassian/Isaac will take another swipe at it in 10.14.3. See Conrad Leyser, "*Lectio divina, oratio pura*: Rhetoric and the Techniques of Asceticism in the *Conferences* of John Cassian," in *Modelli di santità e modelli di comportamento: Contrasti, intersezioni, complementarità*, ed. Giulia Barone, Marina Caffiero, and

Francesco Scorza (Turin: Rosenberg e Sellier, 1994), 79–105, at 88.

42. This is the specific meaning of "spiritual knowledge" / *spiritalis scientia* here: Stewart, *Cassian the Monk*, 91.

43. Cassian/Nesteros are referring to the different layers of scriptural meaning that they had discussed in *Collationes* 14.8 (not included here): the historical or literal meaning on the one hand, and, on the other, the deeper meanings encoded in the same passages that involved layers of ethical guidance (tropology), prefiguration of Christian history (allegory), and insights into the afterlife (anagogy).

44. Since Nesteros is addressing monks specifically here, he's probably referring to the Christian practice of opening the Bible at random for oracular guidance to a particular problem, or overhearing a chance recitation of scripture and taking it as a sign of something else. Even the famous monk Antony had practiced bibliomancy—or at least, his hagiographer suggested as much: Robert Wiśniewski, *Christian Divination in Late Antiquity* (Amsterdam: Amsterdam University Press, 2020), 89–104.

45. In theory, Romans learned their ABC's in primary school (*ludus litterarius*) and moved on to poetry

in grammar school (*schola grammatici*). But educational systems varied across the empire, and in practice the pedagogies often blurred together: Robert A. Kaster, "Notes on 'Primary' and 'Secondary' Schools in Late Antiquity," *Transactions of the American Philological Association* 113 (1983): 323–46.

46. *Conversio* could mean converting to monasticism specifically, which is probably what Cassian and Germanus mean here, or converting to Christianity more generally.

47. Abraham is taking a stringent position here. Self-sufficiency was a core value in Egyptian monasticism, but most monks still relied on the support of lay patrons, even if they stressed that they were not beholden to them: Peter Brown, *Treasure in Heaven: The Holy Poor in Early Christianity* (Charlottesville: University of Virginia Press, 2016), 71–108. Via Abraham, Cassian was also critiquing more moderate positions in Gaul: Goodrich, *Contextualizing Cassian*, 151–98; Peter Brown, *Through the Eye of a Needle: Wealth, the Fall of Rome, and the Making of Christianity in the West, 350–550 AD* (Princeton, NJ: Princeton University Press, 2012), 414–19.

48. As Stewart notes (*Cassian the Monk*, 139–40), Abraham is referring to the mountainous Mons Porphyrites / Jabal Abu Dukhān, located between the Nile and the Red Sea in Egypt's Eastern Desert.
49. This work would have been done by carpenters, who built timber-framed centering prior to the installation of structural masonry. The framework would be removed after the stone was laid or the concrete had cured and the ceiling was decorated: Rabun Taylor, *Roman Builders: A Study in Architectural Process* (Cambridge: Cambridge University Press, 2003), 174–211; Ulrich, *Roman Woodworking*, 172–77.
50. Cassian's construction metaphors aren't always precise (see, e.g., 9.2.1), but he may be referring here to the fact that builders would have had to construct both the internal centering and an external form to mold the concrete of the dome (Taylor, *Roman Builders*, 199)—just as a person has to orient both their thoughts and their actions to a single divine reference point.
51. Hunting was an elite sport; the philosopher can't believe that John is debasing himself by coddling a game animal rather than hunting it. But the joke

is on him, because the story plays on a sense of reverse snobbery in late antique ascetic culture: monks and philosophers weren't supposed to hunt in the first place. See, e.g., Thomas Szabó, "Die Kritik der Jagd — Von der Antike zum Mittelalter," in *Jagd und höfische Kultur im Mittelalter*, ed. Werner Rösener (Göttingen: Vandenhoeck und Ruprecht, 1997), 167–229, at 170–75.